The Story of Eng

A History of English Banking, and a Sketch of the Money Market

Henry Warren

Alpha Editions

This edition published in 2024

ISBN : 9789362997432

Design and Setting By
Alpha Editions
www.alphaedis.com
Email - info@alphaedis.com

As per information held with us this book is in Public Domain.
This book is a reproduction of an important historical work. Alpha Editions uses the best technology to reproduce historical work in the same manner it was first published to preserve its original nature. Any marks or number seen are left intentionally to preserve its true form.

Contents

CHAPTER I. The Period of Monopoly, 1708 to 1826. ....- 1 -

CHAPTER II. Before and After the Act of 1844. ....- 11 -

CHAPTER III. The Bank's Weekly Return. ....- 22 -

CHAPTER IV. The Issue and Banking Departments Combined. ....- 30 -

CHAPTER V. The Store in the Issue Department. ....- 36 -

CHAPTER VI. Weekly Differences in the Return. ....- 41 -

CHAPTER VII. The Bank of England as Agent of the Mint. ....- 46 -

CHAPTER VIII. The Principal Currency Drains. ....- 49 -

CHAPTER IX. Banks and the Creation of Credit. ....- 55 -

CHAPTER X. The Battle of the Banks. ....- 61 -

CHAPTER XI. The London Money Market. ....- 67 -

CHAPTER XII. The Bank Rate and Stock Exchange Securities. ....- 73 -

CHAPTER XIII. The Banks as Stockbrokers. ....- 76 -

CHAPTER XIV. The Short Loan Fund and the Price of Securities. ....- 80 -

CHAPTER XV. Panic Years. ....- 84 -
CHAPTER XVI. The Banks and the Public. ....- 104 -
CHAPTER XVII. Bank Stock. ....- 111 -

CHAPTER I.
THE PERIOD OF MONOPOLY, 1708 TO 1826.

THE Bank of England, which is managed by a Governor, Sub-Governor, and twenty-four Directors, was incorporated in 1694 at the suggestion of a Scotsman, William Paterson, a man of roving disposition, whose Darien expedition proved a miserable fiasco, cost Scotland some £400,000, and shattered the health of Paterson, who died in London at the beginning of 1719, if not in poverty at least stripped of nearly all his fortune.

Schemes relating to the Isthmus of Darien (or Panama), that narrow little strip of land which unites the two Americas, have proved fruitful in disaster. France's great canal venture, we all remember, resulted in huge loss and grave scandal; and Paterson lived to bitterly regret his colonisation scheme, devoutly wishing that he had pinned his faith to his finance company, the Bank of England, for a finance company it then was in every sense of the word.

Little is known of William Paterson's early career, the various accounts relating thereto being meagre and conflicting, his enemies describing him as a mere adventurer, and his friends declaring that he was actuated by the worthiest of motives. However, when it is remembered that his second great venture (the Darien scheme) involved thousands in ruin, it is evident that had the man been a saint he would not have lacked detractors, and though his public utterances sound quaintly pious to the modern ear, it seems probable that he was only an enterprising merchant, whose morality was neither better nor worse than that of the times in which he lived.

The son of a Scotch farmer, Paterson left home at an early age, and, after settling for a short time in the West of England, set sail for the West Indies, returning to Europe about 1686 with the Darien scheme in his brain. Receiving but scant encouragement in England, despite the fact that his bank had been successfully floated, he concentrated his energies upon Scotland, where his scheme fired the public imagination, almost every Scotsman with a few pounds to invest eagerly taking the money to the company, convinced that Panama was the natural commercial centre of the world, and that gold would be rained therefrom upon fortunate Scotland. The whole nation went almost frantic with the fever, for Panama, with its gold mines and its world-wide trade, was going to make Scotland rich beyond the dreams of avarice. It is estimated that nearly half the capital of the country was sunk in the Darien scheme.

Chartered by the Scottish Parliament in 1695, three vessels sailed from Leith in July, 1698, with some twelve hundred settlers on board, Paterson and his wife among the number. All Edinburgh flocked down to Leith to wish the members God-speed, and then returned to their homes to dream of the streams of gold with which Scotland was to be flooded. In a few years everybody would be rich, and Edinburgh would be the greatest and proudest city in the world. Trade, however, was destined to flow to a city a little farther south.

The scheme proved a dismal failure. England and Holland opposed the new colony; the East India Company treated it as a rival, and Spain was actively hostile. The climate did the rest. Before the close of 1699 "New Edinburgh" was deserted, and the colonists, decimated by want of provisions and disease, set sail for New York. To make matters worse, a second company meanwhile had sailed from Scotland, where the utmost enthusiasm still prevailed; but the new arrivals found the town deserted, and themselves at the mercy of the Spanish warships. Mad with rage at the lack of success of their national adventure, the Scotch openly accused the English Government of treachery, declaring that its conduct in withholding food supplies was as discreditable to it as was the butchery of Mac Ian and his clan at Glencoe in 1692, when neither old man nor child was spared, and fugitives were allowed to perish of hunger and exposure in the mountains.

Paterson's faith in Panama must have been profound. His wife died in the new colony, and he himself suffered severely in health; yet, after his return towards the end of 1699, directly his health began to improve, we read of his approaching William with a fresh Darien venture. The King naturally refused to risk a second disaster, and Paterson, like all great speculators who have risked everything and lost, could not again persuade the public to share his enthusiasm, for that mysterious entity seldom trusts a man after a cloud has obscured his "star." Once his spell of so-called good luck is broken, the public desert him in a body, when the adventurer, if he be wise, retires into obscurity with his spoil.

Paterson lived to discover that it is only a rising star, radiating success, that can obtain a sufficiently large following to finance a great scheme, and though he strove manfully to promote the new venture, his sanguine predictions were received sceptically. Nor did his subsequent schemes meet with a better reception. But he must still have retained some influence, for, after the Act of Union in 1707, he was returned to Parliament by a Scotch burgh. His chief claim to distinction, however, undoubtedly rests upon the fact that he founded the Bank of England, of which he was appointed one of the first directors.

The Bank of England, from its inception down to the present day, has never been a Government institution. It was originally simply a company that advanced money to and transacted business for the Government, which, in return, granted it certain privileges and concessions; but the connection between the Government and the Bank was so close, and their interests so identical, that public opinion connected the one indissolubly with the other. From this conception sprang the erroneous impression that the Bank is a Government establishment, when, in reality, it is no more so than is the National Provincial Bank of England or the London and County Bank.

In 1694, the Government of William III., which was generally in a state of monetary tightness, found that the war with France was draining its resources, and, having failed to raise sufficient funds by the imposition of taxes, it resolved, apparently as a kind of *dernier ressort*, to accept Paterson's financial scheme, which had been shelved some three years earlier; and on 27th July, 1694, a charter was granted to the "Corporation of the Governor and Company of the Bank of England."

The capital of the company, £1,200,000, was subscribed by some forty London merchants, and lent to the Government. It is only reasonable to assume that the subscribers were supporters of the Government, and that they were Whigs, whose aim, in supplying William with the sinews of war, was the crushing of James, whose pusillanimity had disgusted even his own followers at the battle of the Boyne in 1690.

Then, again, the commercial morality of the Stuarts was notoriously bad in the City. Charles I., when the City of London refused him a loan, took forcible possession of £200,000 deposited by the Goldsmiths in the Exchequer; and Charles II., in 1672, robbed them of considerably over £1,000,000. The Goldsmiths, in those days, were the private bankers with whom the London merchants left their cash, receiving an acknowledgment or receipt in return, promising payment on demand, and the Goldsmiths deposited their surplus cash in the Exchequer, just as the banks of to-day do with the Bank of England. Through this act of spoliation the Goldsmiths were unable to meet their liabilities, and many of them, together with their customers, were involved in common ruin in consequence. James II. added to the financial sins of his house by debasing the currency: so small wonder that the merchants of London had had enough of the Stuarts, whose theory of the "Divine right" of kings did not even stop short at the pockets of their subjects—always their most vulnerable point.

The Bank of England, which to-day is quite outside party politics, was at its inception a Whig finance company, incorporated solely for the purpose of lending its capital to the Government at the rate of eight per cent. per annum; and out of this creation has evolved the present "Old Lady of Threadneedle Street," whose career, if chequered, has been one of unquestionable integrity.

It is difficult even in imagination to picture to oneself the England of 1694; but it is easy to understand that in those days great storehouses of capital were non-existent—non-existent, that is to say, in the modern sense. Our huge credit institutions, which are indispensable in the twentieth century for the proper carrying on of trade, and which dive by means of branches into almost every corner of the land, thereby collecting millions of pounds of loanable capital, would have spread their tentacles in vain during the seventeenth century, when neither the money nor the facilities for its profitable employment existed in the country.

Capital was scarce—consequently the rate of interest was high—and eight per cent. was a rate at which even the Government could not borrow in the City in 1694, from ten to thirteen per cent. per annum being about the value of loanable capital, while the commission paid was oftentimes exorbitant. The Bank, which was established by the Whigs, was naturally bitterly opposed by the Tories, who saw in its success the destruction of the cause they had at heart. The capitalist class disliked it for selfish reasons; and the Goldsmiths, recognising a formidable opponent, joined issue with its enemies.

Holders of stock and everybody connected with the Bank were looked upon as enemies of the House of Stuart, which, were it restored to power, would naturally wreak its vengeance upon a company that had helped to finance William—for forgiveness is one of those abstract attributes with which only brave and wise men are blest, and James II. had not given proof of possessing either courage or wisdom. Small wonder then that the City should support the Dutchman.

The National Debt, too, was founded during the reign of William, the first loan of £1,000,000 being raised in 1693, and those persons who held it were bound by the strongest of ties—commercial ties—to William. The fund-holders were Liberal; the Bank was Liberal; and as its very life was dependent upon the existence of the Government, it seems only natural that, in the popular mind, it should have been looked upon as a Government institution, though there is but little excuse for so classing it now. The fact that so many people still share this illusion, however, clearly proves that a large proportion of the public is unacquainted with the Bank's history.

The Bank of England's charter was renewed in 1697, and again in 1708, when, in order to prevent the establishment of similar institutions, it was granted the monopoly of Joint Stock Banking in England. This it retained until 1826, when an Act was passed permitting the formation of Joint Stock Banks of Unlimited Liability beyond sixty-five miles of London, provided they had no branches in the Metropolis.

It is a long jump from 1708 to 1826, and, of course, the charter was renewed many times between the two dates, the Government generally taking advantage of each extension to force some concession from the Bank, which, as its credit and business expanded, had increased its original capital by many millions; but 1826 was the year of reform, and the intervening period possesses little interest except to the student.

Between 1826 and 1829 the Bank opened eleven provincial branches, but those which were established at Gloucester, Swansea, Exeter, and Norwich have since been closed. Joint Stock Banks were then started in the provinces, though not with very happy results, for in 1832 their reckless trading was severely stigmatised by Lord Overstone; but it was not until 1834 that the first joint stock bank, the London and Westminster, was started in London, a clause having been inserted in the Act when the charter of the Bank of England was renewed in 1833, to the effect that, provided a joint stock bank did not issue notes, it was at liberty to carry on business in the City.

Both the Bank of England and the London private bankers opposed the new bank with acerbity, the former refusing to open an account for it in its books, and the latter declining to admit it into the Clearing House. Not satisfied with this, the Bank brought an action against the Westminster. But it was quite natural that the newcomer should have been received in this fashion, for innovations, however necessary and useful, are seldom accepted rapturously in this country, which appears to have almost a Chinese dislike of the unusual. Besides, it is not the custom of the country, even for the sake of appearances, to receive a trade rival with open arms, and it would have been a little surprising had the Bank surrendered its monopoly of joint stock banking in England without a struggle, whilst its desire, after being stripped of some of its privileges, to annoy its despoilers, was, if not laudable, eminently human.

In 1836 the London Joint Stock Bank followed the example of the Westminster, and in 1839 the Union Bank of London, which has recently amalgamated with Messrs. Smiths, opened its doors, while such well-known banks as the National Provincial Bank of England and the London and County Bank were formed in 1833 and 1836 respectively. The trade of the country had by that time far outgrown the resources of the Bank of

England, which was quite unable to minister to the increasing demands of a prosperous and progressive England; and to-day the only monopoly which the Bank enjoys is that left to it by the Act of 1844.

From William and Mary to Victoria, in whose reign the Act of 1844—that Magna Charta of the banking community—was introduced, covers a most interesting period in the history of the nation, whose development had been retarded by the "Divine right" of the Stuarts, which cost Charles I. his head and James II. his throne. The theory is much in evidence to-day, though it now takes the form of a great abstract idea, not compatible with practical politics, and which has found a resting place in the heart, rather than in the head, of the people—for the practical twentieth century has a strange trick of banishing disproved theories from the head to the heart; and perhaps it is this national trait which saves the country from violent revolutions.

It would be a mistake to assert that commerce had declined under the Stuarts. It increased rapidly in spite of them; but, after the "Glorious Revolution," the "Divine right" of kings became a mere theory in this country, and the power of the Crown was made subservient to the will of the people. In short, the rule of Parliament began. The trade of the country gradually expanded, and with it the influence of the Bank.

In order that we may thoroughly grasp the position previously occupied by the Bank of England, and the influence given to it by its connection with the Government, it will be better, before briefly discussing the Act of 1844, to revert to the days when the sway of the Bank of England was absolute.

In 1708, we know, the Bank was granted the monopoly of joint stock banking in England, and, further, it was made illegal for any private firm, whose partners were more than six in number, to conduct the business of a banker. This restriction was not removed until 1857, when the partners in a private bank might consist of ten, and it will be seen from the following facts that this limitation was harmful to the best interests of the country.

One result of this hard-and-fast enactment was the encouragement of small private banks in every county of England; but the fact that the number of their partners was limited to six effectually checked their expansion, and finally brought hundreds of them to the ground; for they could not strengthen themselves, and add to their resources, by amalgamation as is now possible.

As the population of the country increased, the position of the private bankers, as a class, became precarious, especially in rapidly growing commercial centres, because their supply of loanable capital was insufficient to meet the increasing demands of their clients. In their attempt to finance their customers they neglected to maintain adequate reserves, and consequently failures were numerous directly any very considerable demand was made upon them.

Instead of a few large and powerful banking companies, there existed numerous weak private firms, which, in many instances, had advanced out of all proportion to their total working resources, thereby sacrificing security to large profits. So long as times were good all went merrily; but, unfortunately, the great impetus given to trade by the conclusion of peace with France and the United States in 1783 did not last more than five or six years.

The year 1789 brings us to the French Revolution, and in 1793 we were at war with France again. Then came the reaction. Country bankers failed in every direction; but in 1797 Mr. Pitt came to the rescue in order to relieve the Bank of England, and the directors of the Bank were allowed to issue notes at their discretion, cash payments being suspended. Between 1792 and 1820 over one thousand private bankers put up their shutters; and during the 1825 crisis sixty-five banks closed their doors, hundreds of their customers being ruined in consequence. The panic of 1825, which almost emptied the Bank's tills, thoroughly convinced the Government that the country had outgrown the monopoly of the Bank of England.

By limiting the partners in private banking companies to six in number, and prohibiting the establishment of joint stock banks in opposition to the Bank of England, the Government sanctioned a policy which could not but result in disaster. Like most monopolies, that of the Bank of England was framed to exclude powerful rivals, and to keep those in opposition small and weak; and the result was disaster and ruin in every direction. The greater the trade of the country, the more apparent became the evil, until even the Government was compelled to decide that the monopoly of the Bank of England must forthwith be curtailed.

Small tradesmen were quick to realise the possibilities attached to an unlimited issue of notes, and hundreds of them combined the business of banking with their retail trades, for, although the law placed every obstacle in the way of sound banking, it encouraged small men, who possessed little or no capital, to engage in a business which should be conducted with much capital and great caution. The country was flooded with the notes of these so-called bankers, who, directly their notes were presented for payment in large numbers, failed by the dozen.

A system which encouraged all that was bad, and excluded everything that was sound and secure, was naturally doomed to extinction; and small wonder that in 1826 the era of country joint stock banking began. Like most fresh ventures which cannot be guided by precedent, it began disastrously, for the simple reason that those who were responsible for the guidance of the new companies had to learn from experience—a very bitter school. But the new banks laboured under fewer disadvantages than the old private bankers, and the Bank Act of 1844, we shall see, clearly defined their position.

We can now understand why the private banker was never a great success in this country. He was of course sacrificed to the monopoly of the Bank of England; for although six very rich capitalists could conduct a large banking business, the resources at their command would not be sufficient to enable them to extend their branches throughout the country. Consequently, before the advent of the joint stock banks we find the private banker, broadly speaking, confining his connections to a particular district or county.

It is true that he enjoyed free trade in banking down to 1844; but the regulation as to the number of partners in his business necessarily confined his offices or branches to a limited area, and effectually prevented his expansion on a large scale; so we get influential houses in the various counties, such as the Gurneys in Norfolk and Suffolk, the Smiths in Nottingham, and so on. It is noticeable, however, that both these well-known private firms, recognising the applicability of the joint stock system to the times, have surrendered their note issues, and taken a place in the modern movement, evidently foreseeing that, in order to progress, they must adopt the methods of their more successful rivals.

Undoubtedly, the country was not ripe for such a movement until the beginning of the nineteenth century; and though the number of partners in private banking firms was extended to ten in 1857, this concession by no means placed the private banker on an equal footing with the joint stock companies, which could increase their members or partners by the issue of additional capital whenever it became apparent that their business was rapidly progressing. The private banker, had he desired to farm some dozen counties, would have been compelled to find a few large capitalists to join hands with him, whereas the joint stock banks had only to obtain hundreds of very small ones, and it is quite evident that the companies possessed infinitely the easier task. In fact, down to 1844 the monopoly of the Bank of England prevented their rapid growth. Then came the period of, so to speak, free banking; but not for the private firms.

People are constantly asking: Why did not the private bankers establish themselves firmly in the country and progress? They were first in the field, and, had they been well managed, surely they would have been as progressive as their joint stock rivals.

But we know that the law never gave them the remotest chance. How could they progress on a really gigantic scale when their partners were limited to six? The law literally forced them to stand aside; and in 1826 and 1833 only the joint stock system profited by the concessions wrung from the Bank of England, because by that system alone could sufficient capital be obtained to enable a bank to farm the country from south of the Tweed to Land's End.

Of course the private banker was at liberty to adopt the joint stock system at an earlier date, but he did not at first believe in the new movement, and, consequently, clung to his own system until he was far outdistanced by his competitors, for directly the country was relieved from the incubus in the shape of the Bank of England's monopoly, and the joint stock system was given a free hand, that system, as might have been expected, instantly began to forge ahead, and in a very short space of time the private banker, who to this day cannot admit more than ten persons into partnership, was left hopelessly behind by a system which was unfettered by legal restrictions and allowed fair play.

The Bank of England's monopoly reduced the private banker to impotency. It fostered in every county of England dangerously small firms, which disappeared in hundreds as soon as credit became bad and a state of panic caused their notes to be presented for payment in unusually large numbers, and it made really great private banking companies impossible in England; while but for the fact that public opinion wrenched this power from the hands of the directors, the Bank and its monopoly, which encouraged a dangerous form of banking, might both have been swept away in a bad financial crisis.

Fortunately, public opinion won the day; and though the private banker could not compete successfully against the joint stock system on account of the smallness of his capital compelling him to concentrate his energies in a particular district, that system, being unrestricted, soon covered the land with its branches. The private bankers were at first held in check by the Bank of England's monopoly. Now they are simply being smothered out of existence by the extension of a system of which, in a manner, though, of course, not in the modern sense, the Bank was the first exponent; for a banker, at the beginning of the nineteenth century, was largely dependent upon his note circulation for his profit, our present system of deposit banking being then in its infancy. In fact, the one evolved out of the other.

If a person held one hundred pounds in bank notes, it could not but occur to him that he was in reality lending the issuer one hundred pounds entirely free of interest; and as he possessed sufficient confidence in the banker to lock up the notes in his cash box, it was only going one step farther to deposit his money at his bank and draw out the cash as he required it. Obviously, too, if he exchanged the notes for a deposit receipt, he would receive some interest upon his money; and as the receipt could be held equally as safely as the notes, he naturally adopted the plan that was the more profitable to himself. So, although in 1826 the joint stock banks in the country attached great importance to their circulation, their notes rather took the form of an advertising medium for attracting deposits, or, at least, became a means to that end, for the progressive banks did not hesitate to sacrifice their note issues in order that they might open branches in London.

We find, then, that the joint stock banks at first attempted to place as many of their notes as possible among the public, and that, by the process already explained, the holders of their notes gradually began to deposit with them, until, by degrees, our present system of deposit banking obtained a firm hold upon the habits of the people. As the trade of the country expanded, the cheque rapidly drove out a large proportion of the bank notes in circulation; and though the issue of notes certainly introduced deposit banking in this country, modern requirements have made cheques and bills of exchange the media for the transference of credit. Such being the case, the note issues of the larger joint stock banks became of secondary importance to them; and, rather than remain outside the Metropolis, we have seen that they sacrificed their notes to the monopoly of the Bank of England.

From 1708 to 1826 the Bank of England owed its predominant position entirely to monopoly, and enough has been written to show that its sway was not an unmixed blessing to the country. The private banker, without a shadow of doubt, can trace his lack of progress to the restrictions placed upon his business by the Bank charter; and the joint stock companies may certainly be said to have succeeded in spite of the Bank; yet no greater compliment can be paid to any institution than to assert that it has earned the respect, if not the love, of its enemies; and such undoubtedly may be truthfully affirmed of the "Old Lady of Threadneedle Street," even when her rule was autocratic and her rivals' dislike of her intense.

CHAPTER II.
BEFORE AND AFTER THE ACT OF 1844.

WE have seen that part of the Bank of England's monopoly was annulled in 1826, and that in 1833 a clause was inserted in the charter to the effect that joint stock banks of unlimited liability could open in London, provided they did not issue notes; and though the state of the law still allowed the Bank to harass and annoy the new companies, its power was thoroughly broken, and its monopoly of joint stock banking gone—fortunately for ever.

The country enjoyed a period of prosperity from 1833 to 1836, but the speculative fever soon began to develop, and by the end of 1835 it was burning fiercely, for men and women possessed an extraordinary faith in those much advertised short cuts to wealth in the early thirties. No path, if it were sufficiently short, was too precipitous. Hope was boundless, credit was unlimited, and companies in profusion were formed by the philanthropists and dreamers of those times.

Then came the crisis of 1837, when the Bank's policy rose almost to the verge of madness. Just at a critical moment, when it was imperative that no untoward incident should occur to disturb the already depressed state of credit, the Bank of England refused, and persisted in its refusal, to discount bills bearing the endorsement of the joint stock banks.

The action of the Bank added to the confusion, and, as speculation in America had been rampant, it dealt a final blow to the houses engaged in the American trade by issuing instructions that their bills also should not be discounted. Then, as might have been expected, the fury of the storm beat against the Bank itself; and by the end of February, 1837, its bullion was reduced to £4,077,000. In 1839 another crisis occurred, and the bullion declined to £2,522,000. Upon this occasion £2,500,000 was borrowed from the Bank of France, and the discount rate of the Bank of England was gradually advanced to six per cent.

These constantly recurring panics thoroughly alarmed the Government, which, having stripped the Bank of England of its monopoly of joint stock banking, now turned its attention to the currency, and by the Bank Act of 1844 secured the convertibility of the note. In fact, the chief aim of the Act was to reduce the issues of the country bankers, who, by forcing large numbers of their one pound notes into circulation and neglecting to maintain a sufficient proportion of cash in hand to meet them on presentation, helped to finance the gamble of 1824. Some of the banks paid the penalty in the year following, and disappeared from the scene.

In 1821 the Bank of England, after a period of restriction, began to pay off its notes under the value of £5, but the Government allowed the country bankers to continue issuing their small notes until the expiry of the Bank Charter in 1833. In 1826 an Act was passed prohibiting the stamping of notes under £5, and forbidding the circulation after April, 1829, of those then current.

The Bank Act of 1844 confirmed the alterations of 1826 and 1833, and, in addition, made great alterations in connection with the currency. The Issue Department of the Bank of England was to be kept entirely distinct from the Banking Department. Notes, to the extent of £14,000,000, might be issued against the debt owing by the Government to the Bank and against other securities, but coin and bullion must be deposited in the Issue Department against every note issued in excess of that sum.

Notes issued by the Bank of England are, therefore, secured principally by specie, and by the Government debt, which amounts (1902) to £11,015,100; and as every note is a warrant entitling the holder to gold on demand, a Bank of England note is really and truly equivalent to gold. However, under certain possible, if improbable, conditions, the Bank could not fulfil its obligations or promises to pay cash on presentation, for if all its notes in circulation were presented simultaneously there would not be sufficient coin in the Issue Department to meet them; but that is a most unlikely contingency.

Further, these notes are "legal tender" in England. In other words, a debtor can compel his creditor to accept them in discharge of his debt; but nobody is obliged to give out change should the value of the notes tendered exceed the amount of the sum owing. In Scotland and Ireland Bank of England notes are "current" but not "legal" tender. Neither are they by the Bank itself, nor by any of its branches, and sovereigns, though not half-sovereigns or silver, may be demanded in exchange. All notes are convertible at the London Office of the Bank, whose branches, however, are only responsible for those notes issued therefrom.

The Bank still retains the monopoly of issuing notes in London and at a distance not greater than sixty-five miles from the Metropolis. No new bank of issue may be formed; and as the private bankers in London had ceased circulating their notes prior to 1844, the Act practically gave the Bank the monopoly of note issue within the prescribed area. This monopoly alone is of great value; but when we remember that its notes are legal tender in England as well, it is evident that the Bank of England still enjoys a most important concession.

The private bankers of London, and the joint stock banks in London and within sixty-five miles of it, were debarred by the Act of 1844 from issuing notes. Of course the private bankers who still issued notes within the prescribed space retained their privilege, but they were no longer able to circulate as many as they could persuade the public to accept.

Bankers, both joint stock and private, who claimed the privilege of issuing notes were compelled to make a return of their issues for a period of twelve weeks to a given date, when the average amount was ascertained, and the extent of the future issue of each bank settled in accordance therewith. The issues, in other words, were fixed, and they could not exceed the sum authorised without breaking the law, and exposing themselves to a fine equivalent to the average excess during any one month. The Government, anxious to avoid a repetition of the scandals of 1825 and 1836, was evidently determined to limit the note circulations of the country banks, and there seems little doubt that, when the Act was framed, one of its aims was the slow but sure extermination of the country bank note.

Banks which intend giving up their note circulations may compound with the Bank of England, which is then allowed to increase its own issue by two-thirds of the disappearing issues. The Government, however, takes all the profit accruing from such arrangements.

The result of these regulations can be seen in the accretions made from time to time to the Bank's authorised issue of £14,000,000, which has now increased to £18,175,000. The majority of the issues of the private bankers fixed by the Act of 1844 have since lapsed; and the same may be said of the more progressive of the country joint stock banks, which, as their deposits grew, opened branches in London, thereby sacrificing their note circulations to the monopoly of the Bank of England, whose notes are fast driving those of the small country bankers out of circulation. Broadly speaking, it may be said that Bank of England notes are the only notes accepted readily by the English public; but the mere fact of their being legal tender ensures that.

Readers who are not acquainted with the history of Banking must not assume that the Act of 1844 affects either Scotland or Ireland. The note circulation of both those countries is regulated by the Act of 1845, but in neither country are the provisions identically the same as those affecting England.

Any person may demand of the Issue Department notes in exchange for gold bullion of standard fineness at the rate of £3 17s. 9d. per ounce.

The Bank Act of 1844, according to its framers, would make panics and crises evils of the past; but, as a matter of fact, it was a new broom, and its sweeping powers were greatly overestimated. Its provisions, we can see, related entirely to currency reform; and though the country bankers could no longer borrow on their notes to an unlimited extent, it must be remembered that Sir Robert Peel's famous Act, if it fixed the maximum amount of their issues, did not take the precaution to also fix the minimum reserve of cash in hand to be held against them. Obviously, no Act could strengthen the position of the banks against panics unless it laid down the minimum or legal reserve of cash to be maintained against deposits, and we shall see that, in this respect, the Act of 1844 did not realise expectations.

Controversy raged furiously around Peel's Act, and, needless to say, it became the bone of party contention. Whenever a subject reaches that stage in this country, its merits are forced into the background. Sides are taken, critics and politicians range themselves upon either the one or the other, and the subject, consequently, speedily gets all the truth lashed out of it. The number of people who really understand the question thoroughly is infinitesimal; and they, as a rule, by a strange irony of fate, do not dabble in politics. The important subject is therefore handed over to the tender mercies of the multitude, which, quite ignorant of its underlying principles, splits itself into two hostile camps, beats out the dust with sticks, and then returns a man to Parliament to vote on this side or on that.

When in 1847, three years after the passing of the Act, another crisis occurred, public opinion attached all the blame to Peel's Act; but public opinion was wrong. Public opinion is usually based upon instinct rather than upon reason, and, consequently, carried away by a sense of indignation or wrong, it rushes madly at what it considers the cause of the mischief. In this case its bugbear was Peel's Act. The real reason was to be found in the simple fact that neither the Bank of England nor any of the large banks held a sufficient proportion of cash in hand to meet those sudden demands for gold which may be made upon a banker at any moment, and to which his business is peculiarly exposed during periods of bad credit.

It was the old, old story, which in these days seems hardly to require an explanation. After a period of exceptional prosperity, there almost invariably follows a lean year or two, when loanable capital is cheap and the prices of commodities depressed. Then is the company promoter's opportunity, and schemes, wise and otherwise, are brought to the notice of the public. Presently there comes a gradual expansion of enterprise, and rising prices beget confidence, when a whisper goes round to the effect that good times are coming.

At first business improves slowly and surely. Then, as prices mount higher and higher, every producer increases his output, anxious to share in the general prosperity. Suddenly, just before the end, there is a boom. Prices rush madly upwards, until every prudent man sees that business has degenerated into a mere gamble, and that he must act quickly if he does not wish to be caught by the receding tide. Unless the banks are strong at that moment, disaster is inevitable; and as they had not taken the necessary precaution in 1847, the result was a crisis.

Capital was cheap during the last quarter of 1844, the Bank rate remaining stationary at two-and-a-half per cent. from September of that year to October, 1845. Cheap money gives the promoter his opportunity; and in 1845 the railway mania was at its zenith. England was in the hands of the surveyor, and the "boom" began in real earnest. As usual, everybody was to become immensely rich, and, as usual, most people were again bitterly disappointed. By a strange process of reasoning, experience does not count in finance. Hope, after a very little while, drives out of the memory of human beings the nightmare of disaster; so, in an astonishingly short space of time, they are gambling again. The crisis of 1837 had lost all its significance by 1845; and then, of course, the Bank Act was to prevent commercial panics in the future!

At the end of 1846 the Bank rate was raised to four per cent., and in October, 1847, it touched eight per cent. The speculation in railways naturally resulted in a gamble in iron; and, after the terrible famine in Ireland of 1846, when thousands died of fever and want in their wretched hovels and even on the roadsides, the suspension of the Corn Laws led to large importations of foreign grain. A sudden fall in prices immediately followed the increased supply, and the merchants in Mark Lane began to fail. Then people looked gravely at one another, and inquired what would happen next.

Credit is the disposition of one person to trust another; therefore as business gradually expands, credit or confidence increases at precisely the same ratio; and when prices are high and profits large, the impression prevails that everybody is making money—consequently, confidence begins to drive out caution; so, towards the end of a period of prosperity the acquisitive fever burns fiercely. Everybody is in mad haste to get rich; caution is flung to the winds; and we get a *débâcle*. Then follows a time of bad credit. That is to say, immediately after the reaction, everyone is disposed to be sceptical of his neighbour's position, to wonder whether he were hit by the recent upheaval, and to be extremely cautious in granting credit to his customers. This took place after the crisis of 1847. For a little while everybody was afraid to trust his neighbour; but by 1857 speculation was in full swing again, and the inevitable collapse followed. These periods of good and bad times, or good and bad credit, run their course with the regularity of a fever.

So it was in 1847. Directly a few failures were announced, the public became alarmed, and speculation received a check. The failures continued, and every holder of bills, anxious to have money at his credit at the banks, tried to discount them. But the banks were totally unprepared for this sudden demand, and in Liverpool and Newcastle some of them closed their doors. The London bankers refused their customers ordinary accommodation, and the Bank of England at first declined to advance against securities. Bills, consequently, could not be met at maturity, and the result was panic and a run on the banks.

The situation was saved by the suspension of the recently passed Bank Act, and on 25th October, 1847, the Government authorised the Bank of England to issue notes at its discretion, until the feeling of apprehension had subsided. The Bank thereupon advanced on bills and stock, and, although the rate of discount was eight per cent., the fact that money could be obtained on good bills and first-class securities speedily allayed the panic, and by 23rd November following the Act was again in force. Further, the amount issued by the Bank beyond the limit imposed thereby did not exceed £400,000, although its reserve, by 23rd October, was reduced to £1,547,000.

Perhaps we shall now be better able to understand the Act of 1844, and to see that, though it effected a most useful reform in the currency, and prevented a host of weak country bankers inundating the provinces with their doubtful paper, it does not contain a single clause which would either prevent or alleviate a panic. Indeed the paradox is that during a crisis relief can only be obtained by breaking the Act, and allowing the Bank of England to advance notes freely against the better-class securities. The power to issue notes was taken out of the hands of numerous weak banks, and confided to one strong one. Perhaps, however, it would be more correct to say that the power for evil of the small country bankers was "fixed" by the Act; and, as we have seen, the Bank of England's notes are gradually driving those of the English provincial banks out of circulation. Then, again, the extinction of the country issues gave a marked impetus to our modern system of deposit banking. The cheque soon became the principal credit document in circulation, and the country joint stock banks relied absolutely for their advancement upon their ability to attract deposits to their books.

So long as the Bank of England's notes can be exchanged for gold on demand, it is impossible for them to depreciate in value, and they cannot drive more gold out of the country than is equal to the Bank's fixed or authorised maximum, because, against every note issued in excess, specie for a like amount must be deposited in the Issue Department. Certain writers urge that this limitation is an interference with the freedom of the banker; but, seeing that our modern system of banking rests upon so small a cash basis, surely it is absolutely essential that our currency at least should be above suspicion in times of falling credit. The public does not require notes then. It wants credit; and this it obtains in the books of the banks.

The currency, certainly, should be left absolutely to the laws of supply and demand; and though it is true that the Bank of England sometimes has to protect the convertibility of its notes by raising its rate of discount, still, our present system approaches very near to perfection in so far as the exchange of the note for gold is concerned, and it certainly does not seem desirable to have the country again flooded with paper money which may, or may not, be paid on presentation.

Any person who possesses gold can have it turned into coin immediately; so, under our present system, every addition to the currency must come either direct from the mines or else be received in settlement of the balance of indebtedness owing by foreign nations to this country. We are, therefore, spared those evils which result from an over-issue of paper, and which were sometimes so greatly in evidence before the passing of the Act of 1844.

The absurdity of the attack on the Act must now be apparent, inasmuch as the only reform it could possibly effect was a currency reform, which was certainly badly needed. Viewed in that light it must surely be acknowledged that the Bank Act of 1844 is one of the soundest financial Bills that has ever become an Act of Parliament. The fact that, in spite of the great change in our banking system—which may be said to have been revolutionised since 1844—the Act has successfully stood the test of time, is also proof positive (if proof were required) that it was framed with great skill and judgment.

Had the Act further decreed that every bank should maintain a ratio of, say, at least eighteen per cent. of legal tender against its public liabilities, even panics might have been avoided. At any rate, the banks would have been better prepared to meet drains upon their resources, though even then—as has been pointed out is the case with the Act itself—the law would have to be broken directly a run was made on the banks by their customers. For all that, such a regulation would keep the banks in a fair state of preparedness during normal times, and consequently every bank in the land would be ready to face a panic.

Our system of credit is based on a small cash reserve; and it would be impossible to devise any workable scheme which would afford bankers absolute security, because it would prove too costly both to the banks themselves and to their customers, who would have to pay much higher rates in proportion as the depositors' money was secured. The most prudent banker can only insure his business up to a certain point, as, if he kept more than a certain proportion of cash in hand, he would conduct his business at a loss; so if a panic take possession of his customers and they rush for gold, he is lost if the demand should drain his reserve and encroach on his till-money. No system in the world could possibly save him then. The most our banks can do, therefore, is to be prepared to a certain extent, and, viewed in the light of past history, it is criminal of directors not to take the ordinary precautions. A clause in the Act, as already suggested, would at least ensure a fair state of preparedness in all our banking companies, and beyond that it is impossible to go.

It has been shown that the Act works most effectively in a time of panic when it is broken. It is, perhaps, interesting to recall that the Bank of Germany, in order to remedy this defect, is allowed to issue notes beyond the authorised amount at its own discretion; but the German Government, in order to check abuses, makes over-issue an unprofitable transaction for the Bank by imposing a fine of five per cent. on any amount issued in excess of the authorised limit. Were our own Government to adopt the same expedient, the Bank of England, during a time of stress and excitement, could meet all demands automatically, and the Act would be almost perfect of itself. On the other hand, the Government might not like to see so much power pass into the hands of the directors of the Bank, though there can be little doubt that they would use it with the greatest moderation and to the public advantage.

The object of this chapter is to show that panics were not lessened in any degree by the Act, and perhaps it may be said that the fact has been dinned into one's ears to the verge of irritation. But an ardent reformer's feelings are strong, and it is difficult to make this subject clear to those who are not conversant with the history of Banking, and who, perhaps, are disposed to think the subject both dry and uninteresting.

The panic of 1847 was followed by another in 1857, and in 1866 the Overend and Gurney crisis occurred. From 1866 down to the present day, unless we include the Baring scare in 1890, the country has been free from these scourges, and the reason is not very far to seek.

The Act of 1844 placed the currency of the country on a sound basis, and experience, by teaching the banks caution, did the rest. The large banking companies, after the terrible panic of 1866, plainly recognised that advances must be made with great discretion, and that, if they valued their own safety, speculation must be either kept well within bounds or discouraged entirely. Merchants and traders who require capital for speculative purposes can only obtain it by making application to the banks, which, in the very great majority of instances, now refuse to make advances unless tangible securities be deposited to cover their loans.

Merchants, therefore, unless their credit be exceptionally good, or unless they possess first-rate stocks and shares, cannot speculate to the same extent as was possible forty years ago and, of course, those persons who possess marketable securities, which bring them in incomes, are the last people in the world to risk an assured position for possible great future gain. They are accustomed to the good things of this earth, and though they may earnestly desire a large accretion to their wealth, the thought that, in the event of failure, they may lose what they already possess, checks the impulse to finance a scheme, which, while holding out promises of great success, is also not without possibilities of grave disaster. As a rule, only small men will take such risks, and the banks will not finance them at any price.

By refusing to accommodate weak speculators, the banks have kept business in a healthy channel, and have largely confined speculation to those people who can afford to pay their losses—always a cautious class. The rank speculator, therefore, has been driven to outside houses, and such houses, we know, are constantly failing; but Lombard Street, having weeded this dangerous element out of its system, is now more stable.

Recognising that their system of credit is always exposed to possible disaster, and having had the fact brought forcibly home to them upon so many occasions, the banks, since 1866, have gradually accumulated larger and larger cash reserves in order to be better prepared to deal immediately and effectively with those cataclysms which from time to time are certain to assail them; and though it is an open question whether their reserves are even now sufficient, the most casual observer must acknowledge that, with a few exceptions, our banking companies are in a better state of preparedness at the moment than perhaps during any other period of their history.

By compelling the schemers to deposit securities against their loans and advances the banks secure themselves against large bad debts; and by accumulating fair cash reserves they insure their business against suspension during panics. Having taken these precautions, it is not surprising that their path has been rendered comparatively smooth during recent years; and, further, the more prudent manner in which the business of a banker is now conducted makes the shares of the large banking companies less speculative holdings, and greatly reduces the risks of shareholders in connection with their liabilities on the uncalled portion of their shares, though that liability should by no means be forgotten or accepted in any other light than that of serious responsibility.

This brings us to another point in their history. It was not until 1858 that banks could be registered as limited liability companies, and, needless to say, no unlimited bank has been formed since that date; whilst every joint stock bank now in existence (although, in the great majority of instances, the members are liable for certain known sums on each share held by them) has limited the liability of its shareholders, those companies formed prior to 1858 having since taken the necessary steps.

Naturally, persons of wealth would not risk their fortunes by holding shares in an unlimited bank, but now that the exact liability is known the responsibility is accepted with a lighter heart, and, consequently, this class of security is considered a desirable investment by those who can afford to take a little risk in return for higher interest than that yielded by the so-called "gilt-edged" variety of securities.

The reader cannot but be struck by the gradual evolution of our banking system; and it must be evident to him that the present more secure position is the outcome of a bitter struggle with adversity. It is usual, when discussing the Bank of England's position in the money market, to degenerate into abuse, and to show that the Old Lady of Threadneedle Street has committed every conceivable folly in dealing with questions of finance. No doubt the accusations are true in the light of past experience. But they were the follies of her times, and, if we are to believe the critics, we are not greatly in advance of our own. Then is it not a little unreasonable to expect the Bank directors of 1825 to be in advance of the financial opinion then current in the City? They had the very best advice of the day at their disposal, and had the present-day critics lived in 1825 they would have urged the Bank directors to take the very course that was then adopted.

English history, at a certain period, seems an account of one long struggle between the will of the people and the power of the Crown; and Banking history, prior to 1844, reads like one long struggle between the banks and the Bank of England. But there is this distinction, to wit, the sterling honesty of the Bank. Surely, in the whole world's history there is not another such instance of unbroken faith on the part of a financial institution which has enjoyed a life of more than two hundred years. While anxious to give an accurate account of the Bank's history, and to explain all its faults and all its failings, it is impossible, the closer one examines its actions, not to be the more impressed by its honesty of purpose.

Every new movement gropes its way out of the darkness into the light. The process is, however, a slow one; and if, in the future, there are new problems to be solved, then future generations will have to learn the laws affecting them in the school of experience. Despite their increased knowledge, they will probably make the same mistakes as those recorded in these chapters, for it is astonishing, as our environment changes, how short a distance we can see in front of our noses. Banking in 1950 will in all probability be very different to banking in 1902—especially if population increases at its present rate all the world over.

CHAPTER III.
THE BANK'S WEEKLY RETURN.

FOR the nonce we have finished with history, and will turn our attention to the Bank of England as it now stands in the centre of the Money Market. The joint stock banks publish their balance sheets either annually or half-yearly; but the Bank of England, in compliance with the Act, compiles a weekly statement to the close of business each Wednesday. This Return or Balance Sheet is submitted to the directors on the following day, and, when passed by them, is exhibited on the wall of the Bank to an expectant crowd of messengers and officials, whose business it is either to criticise or copy it. But by far the greater number of the persons there assembled merely wish to know whether any alteration has been made by the directors in the Bank's discount rate, and, that ascertained, the crowd rapidly thins.

The following is a copy of the Return or Balance Sheet for the week ended Wednesday, 1st October, 1902:—

ISSUE DEPARTMENT.

	£		£
Notes Issued	51,792,330	Government Debt	11,015,100
		Other Securities	7,159,900
		Gold Coin and Bullion	33,617,330
	£51,792,330		£51,792,330

BANKING DEPARTMENT.

LIABILITIES.		ASSETS.	
	£		£

Proprietors' Capital	14,553,000	Government Securities	15,826,080
Rest	3,816,736	Other Securities	31,837,516
Public Deposits (Including Exchequer, Savings' Bank, Commissioners of National Debt, and Dividend accounts)	10,025,973	Notes	21,391,145
Other Deposits	42,695,526	Gold and Silver Coin	2,225,084
Seven-day and other Bills	188,590		
	£71,279,825		£71,279,825
	============		============

A glance at the right hand side of the statement relating to the Issue Department tells us that every note, either in the hands of the public or held in reserve in the Banking Department, is covered by securities and specie deposited in the Issue Department. The amount of the notes in circulation is, of course, obtained by deducting the notes in hand in the Banking Department from the total amount of Notes Issued on the left-hand side of the Issue Department. The difference, £30,401,185, is called the "circulation," and represents the sum which the Bank of England had borrowed from the public on its notes on the 1st October last.

Each department is distinct, and has, in fact, a separate existence; so if the Banking Department requires gold, it must, like an ordinary individual, exchange some of its notes in hand at the Issue Department, obtaining therefrom the additional coin to satisfy the demands of its customers in the Banking Department.

The Bank has transferred the Government debt and other securities, which together amount to £18,175,000, to the Issue Department, and this sum is called the "authorised issue," for the simple reason that the Government allows the Bank to issue notes for a like amount against these securities, which are mortgaged to the holders of its notes. Gold coin and bullion, we know, must be deposited against every note issued in excess of this sum; and as both sides of the statement agree, it is evident that this has been done. These £51,000,000 of gold and securities, then, are hypothecated to the holders of the Bank's notes, and, in the event of the Bank of England being wound up, the creditors in the Banking Department could not touch either the securities or the gold. But we see that the Bank holds £21,391,145 of its own notes in the Banking Department, and, of course, these notes are secured in the same manner as those held by the public; consequently, this department enjoys similar rights and privileges in respect of them. Add the notes in hand in the Banking Department to the "circulation," and it will be found that the total equals the amount issued.

It follows that the Bank only makes a profit on the authorised portion of its note issue, for, as gold is deposited against the remainder, it must lose thereupon to the extent of the cost of production of the notes issued in excess. Obviously, then, the Act does not limit the note issue of the Bank, but it does limit that portion which is not covered by gold, and, consequently, it removes the probability of our seeing Bank of England notes at a discount, as was the case during the early part of the nineteenth century, for the fact that the Bank of England is compelled to redeem its notes in gold on demand prevents depreciation of its paper.

Of course, the amount of notes in circulation varies from day to day, and so, too, does the amount of notes issued, which rises and falls as the stock of bullion in the Issue Department is either increased or diminished. Every note paid is immediately cancelled, and no note, after it has been changed at the Bank, ever goes into circulation again. Hence the reason why Bank of England notes present such a marked contrast to the notes of the country bankers, who issue their paper over and over again, until it becomes quite unpleasant to handle, and distinctly malodorous.

The Bank of England may be said to perform four separate functions. Its Issue Department, as we have seen, is responsible for the notes. Secondly, the Bank manages the National Debt on behalf of the Government. Thirdly, in consequence of its holding the bankers' reserves, it acts as agent for the Mint. And, fourthly, it conducts an ordinary banking business, but it includes among its customers the largest and most influential depositor and borrower in the Kingdom, to wit, the British Government.

The Banking Department, which we will next discuss, stands quite by itself. The first entry on the left-hand side of the balance sheet, we can see, consists of the Bank's capital. Then follows the "rest" or reserve fund, which is never allowed to fall below £3,000,000, the accretions made thereto from time to time representing the profits of the Bank, which are distributed among the stockholders in the shape of dividend after the close of each half-year on the 5th April and the 5th October.

The third entry on the statement, Public Deposits, is made up of the various Government balances; and Other Deposits, which form by far the largest debit in the balance sheet, comprise current account and bankers' balances, the latter largely predominating. Since 1877 the Bank has not published the sum standing to the credit of the London bankers in its books; and as this deposit represents the reserve upon which the bankers might have to draw in the event of a panic, it seems an error of judgment not to give publicity to the figures, even if they do show how largely the Bank of England is dependent upon the other banks for its own working resources.

Public or Government Deposits and Other Deposits stand in a very peculiar relation to each other, and, before discussing the October return, it is perhaps desirable to illustrate this relation. The fiscal year ends on the 5th April; consequently, the Government is busily engaged in collecting the revenue during January, February, and March. "Other Deposits" are often referred to as the market fund of cash, and as those persons who pay their taxes draw cheques upon their bankers, it follows that during these months huge sums are transferred from the bankers' balances (Other Deposits) to the credit of Public Deposits, which are consequently swollen appreciably.

Bankers' balances being reduced, the banks have therefore less to lend; and if the demand for loanable capital is brisk at the time, borrowers are driven to the Bank of England, which sometimes has to raise its rate of discount in order to protect its reserve. Payment of instalments upon Government loans and large issues of Treasury bills produce a like effect.

On the 5th October (four days after the date of the return under discussion) a quarterly instalment on the National Debt is due. Then credit flows from Government Deposits back to Other Deposits. The banks can lend freely again, and the Bank of England, in order to attract borrowers, may even have to lower its rates. Undoubtedly, this is a somewhat artificial state of affairs, because money at times is made either cheap or dear, not solely as the result of demand and supply, but partly according to the personality of the holders of the loanable capital when the demand arises.

A glance at the return shows us that there is a balance of over £10,000,000 against Government Deposits. This implies that the Bank has control of the money market, that many of the bill brokers, finding Lombard Street empty, have been compelled to borrow from the Bank, which puts on the screw as demands upon its resources increase. Further, rates are not likely to be easier until money is released by the Government. Were the banks to keep their own reserves, and did the Government deposit with three or four of the strongest of them, then this constantly recurring tightness would not occur; but under our one reserve system it is unavoidable. However, it by no means follows that the average rate of discount would be lower under such a system. Indeed, the probability is that it would be much higher, because the banks would be compelled to keep larger reserves, and, consequently, would have less to lend.

The last amount on the liability side of the statement is £188,590, which is owing by the Bank on bills in circulation. Shortly after the passing of the Act, and before the joint stock banks had accumulated their vast deposits, the Bank of England issued a much larger volume of these post bills; but since the country banks have been able to draw upon their London agents and head offices in London, the Bank's bills in circulation have gradually dropped from well over £1,000,000 to their present figures. The last three entries, when added together, give us the amount of the Bank's indebtedness to the Government and to the public; and the aggregate, £71,279,825, represents the total liabilities of the Banking Department. But a company, if it be solvent, must possess assets for a like sum, and these we find on the right hand or credit side of the statement.

Nearly £16,000,000 are invested in Government securities; and though any advances made to the Government by the Bank on deficiency bills are included therewith, the description is correct, as a loan to the British Government is as safe as Consols. Just before the dividends on the funds fall due the balance in the Exchequer is often insufficient to meet requirements, and it is then that money is borrowed from the Bank of England on deficiency bills. Of course the Bank also advances to the Government for other purposes, and the extent of these loans may be seen in the statement issued by the Chancellor of the Exchequer each week.

The next entry on the Assets side, "Other Securities," is extremely misleading, or, at least, it embraces such a wide variety of assets as to make the entry practically useless to all who wish to ascertain the real position of the Bank. Included therein are (1) All the investments of the Bank other than Government securities; (2) Loans to customers and to the Stock Exchange, and bills of exchange discounted for customers and for the bill brokers; (3) The book value of its various premises, unless, of course, its head office and branches have been paid for out of the profits of previous years, on which subject the return does not enlighten us.

The balance sheets of some of the minor joint stock banks are disgracefully compiled, but, with respect to this one entry, the Bank of England return runs them very close, and it seems a pity that so powerful a corporation does not set a better example. The Bank, because it holds the bankers' reserves and keeps the Government accounts, is often able to corner the outside market; therefore the least it can do is to issue a plain statement, which will enable the public to see the exact situation created by the unique position it occupies.

The return is badly worded, and essential information is certainly withheld, while distinctness is not by any means one of its good points, for nobody, unless he studied the statement with the greatest care, could possibly divine the meaning of some of its quaint, old-world phraseology. But, as we all know, "great men and great things are never in a 'urry"; and the Bank of England, which is great in the best sense of the word, like the Government whose account it keeps, has never been known to anticipate a new development. A pedigree person always swears by the old. But the time has surely arrived when public opinion should compel the directors to issue a fuller and less ambiguous weekly statement. The present form was no doubt a model of lucidity in 1844; but it is woefully behind the times in 1902.

The last two entries on the Assets side form the Bank's reserve of legal tender. Strictly speaking, a bank's cash reserve is that sum which it has set aside to meet possible demands of an abnormal character, and as the Bank of England's till-money is included in the two entries in question, the total, £23,616,229, cannot be considered a true reserve, as a certain deduction has first to be made therefrom to provide for the ordinary demands made upon its resources in the usual course of business. Further, the Bank, because it is the bankers' bank, is peculiarly exposed to large drains of specie and notes. It follows, therefore, that to ascertain its true reserve, a very large amount would have to be deducted from the sum in question. A true reserve is a sum set apart for a particular purpose, of which no portion is used in the business it is intended to guarantee. It is a fund apart. Consequently, a banker's real reserve is obtained by deducting from his legal tender in hand the sum he requires for the conduct of his business. The Bank of England, however, needs more till-money than an ordinary banking institution.

Glancing at the liability side of the statement, we see that the first two entries represent working capital. In other words, £18,369,736 is a fixed sum, against which it is not necessary to hold one penny in reserve, because no withdrawals can be made therefrom during a time of bad credit. Such an immense amount of working capital makes the Bank of England more independent of its depositors than is the ordinary joint stock bank, and, therefore, its strength as a banking company is increased appreciably thereby, for the weakness of our banking system is due entirely to a fear of possible sudden demands on the part of depositors.

Still keeping on the same side, the last three entries give us the Bank's liabilities to the Government and to the public; and as large demands upon this sum of £52,910,089 may be made at any moment, a sum of notes and coin is held in the Banking Department to meet them. This sum, the Bank's so-called reserve, amounts, we know, to £23,616,229, and we next have to ascertain the ratio per cent. it bears to the liabilities in question. The following sum will supply the answer:

$$(£23,616,229 \times 100) / (£52,910,089) = £44 \cdot 6\%$$

The Bank, then, on 1st October last, held £44·6 in notes and specie in the Banking Department to meet each £100 it owed to its customers. Yet we say "as safe as the Bank of England," when, as a matter of fact, the Bank could not pay its debts on demand; and, paradoxical as it may seem, so the Bank *is* safe, because its credit is so good that no man in England would ever dream of questioning its stability, for, if he did, he would only be laughed at for his pains. Again, comparatively speaking, the Bank of England is certainly safer than its rivals, and when we consider, in so far as its customers are concerned, the huge amount of its capital and reserve, it is evident that it is by far the safest bank in the land for depositors, as the larger the capital of a bank the greater is the guarantee of the customer against loss.

We have seen that the notes and coin in the Banking Department work out at a ratio per cent. of 44·6 to deposits; but as notes are not legal tender by the Bank of England, its creditors can refuse to accept them in discharge of a debt. This £21,391,145 of notes might, however, have been exchanged for gold with the Issue Department at any moment, so that the Bank could have paid off 44·6 per cent. of its liabilities on the day in question—a huge proportion.

It may be objected that, as a certain portion of its gold is held in bars, which would have to be sent to the Mint for coinage, the Bank could not discharge its debts quite so rapidly, and the contention would be perfectly true. But, assuming this exchange were made, £12,226,185 in gold would remain in the Issue Department to meet £30,401,185 of notes in circulation. The Bank, of course, could not then pay one half of its notes were they presented; but such a demand is almost outside the bounds of probability. Still, it is one of those extremely remote possibilities which no prudent Board of Directors can afford to forget; and we may be quite sure that this fact has not been overlooked by the Bank, which can always protect its gold by raising its discount rate.

In the next chapter another view will be taken of the Bank of England's weekly balance sheet.

CHAPTER IV.
THE ISSUE AND BANKING DEPARTMENTS COMBINED.

IN the preceding chapter the Issue and Banking Departments of the Bank of England have been discussed separately. Strictly speaking they can, of course, only be so treated, as each division stands alone; yet the notes in the Banking Department undoubtedly form a connecting link between the two divisions, seeing that they make the one department by far the largest single creditor of the other. Therefore it is intended in this chapter to discuss the return as a whole, to place the totals in the Issue Department back in the Banking Department, and to ascertain the Bank's exact state of preparedness to meet all its liabilities. The following table will enable us to do this:

ISSUE AND BANKING DEPARTMENTS.

	£		£
Capital	14,553,000	Specie and Bullion	35,842,414
Rest or Reserve Fund	3,816,736	Government Debt	11,015,100
Notes in Circulation	30,401,185	Other Securities	7,159,900
Public Deposits	10,025,973	Government Securities	15,826,080
Other Deposits	42,695,526	Loans, Bills Discounted, Securities, etc.	31,837,516
Seven-Day Bills	188,590		
	£101,681,010		£101,681,010

- 30 -

1st October, 1902.

Ratio % of Specie and Bullion to Liabilities.	Ratio % of Investments and Government Debt to Liabilities.	Total Liquid Assets.	Ratio % of Capital to Liabilities.	Ratio % of Rest to Liabilities.	Total Working Capital.	Ratio % of Loans, Bills, etc., to Liabilities.
43·02	40·81	83·83	17·46	4·58	22·04	38·21

It may be urged that as the gold and securities in the Issue Department are mortgaged to the holders of Bank of England notes, they cannot be treated as ordinary assets, and that is true enough; but when we remember that upon the day in question the Banking Department could have exchanged notes to the value of £21,000,000 for gold, the objection loses much of its force.

However, assuming the Banking Department made the exchange, then specie to the extent of over £12,000,000 and the second and third items on the right-hand side of the balance sheet would be mortgaged to the holders of the notes in circulation, and the Bank, were it in need, could legally neither sell the securities nor apply the £12,000,000 in question to the liquidation of any other debt.

But, practically, there is small likelihood of the Bank of England being drained of specie by its notes, which have always been accepted without demur, even during the most troublous years of its history; and, while remembering that the notes in circulation are secured in the manner aforesaid, we may safely consider the Bank's state of preparedness to meet its total public indebtedness from the point of view that its liquid assets would be more than sufficient to discharge all probable demands made by both holders of notes and depositors.

On the 1st October last the Bank owed on its Notes in Circulation, Public and Other Deposits, and Bills, the huge sum of £83,311,274, which we will call its "Liabilities to the Public." Against this it held £35,842,414 in specie and bullion, which, a glance at the table shows, works out at a ratio per cent. of 43·02. The Bank had, then, £43·02 of the precious metals in hand to meet each £100 it owed to its customers. There is not another bank in the kingdom able to publish a balance sheet showing such a splendid proportion of cash in hand to liabilities—but we must also remember that there is not another bank in the country whose responsibilities are so great and so multifarious.

In the previous chapter it was shown that the Banking Department possessed £44·6 in notes and coin to meet each £100 of the public liabilities included therein, and, moreover, this would be the ratio given by the critics; but we now see that, when the two departments are united, the ratio only works out at £43·02. Strictly speaking, the larger ratio is correct; yet the smaller gives a much truer idea of the Bank's ability to pay off its creditors in cash on demand. Further, as the Bank cannot compel its customers to accept its own notes in discharge of a debt, the ratio £43·02 certainly gives one a more accurate impression of the Bank's position in relation to all its creditors.

The Government Debt, Other Securities, and Government Securities amount to £34,001,080, which works out at a ratio per cent. to liabilities of £40·81, making the ratio of total liquid assets £83·83. A debt owing by the British Government is rightly included with the liquid assets of the Bank, for when the credit of the Government ebbs our banking companies, which hold huge amounts of Consols, will no longer be solvent institutions; but no reasonable man imagines that an edifice which has been centuries in building, and which is still far from being either complete or perfect, will "go under" in a day, though all know that it cannot last for ever in its present form. We, however, only live sixty years or so, and therefore each generation of business men considers what will last out its time, and troubles itself but little about what the state of commerce will be fifty years later, as though dimly conscious that, in the end, man will have to go back to the land.

The Bank, we see, possesses £83·83 in cash and the very best securities to meet each £100 it owes to the public. Such figures cannot fail to impress one, for they prove indisputably that, on its merits, the Bank of England is by far the strongest banking company in the three kingdoms. They should not, however, blind our eyes to the fact that the Bank is a credit institution, and that were its creditors to go for gold in a body it would inevitably "smash," for, as we can see from the figures in the first column of the table on page 49, it never keeps a supply of the precious metals equal to its liabilities on demand. But, for all that, the Bank is splendidly prepared to meet every probable demand; and one cannot ask more of its directors.

It would be easy enough to write an indictment against the Bank, proving that its policy is all wrong, that it could not discharge its obligations under certain given conditions, and that, therefore, it is a menace to the solvency of the country. But such deductions, which have already been made by more than one critic, are crass nonsense, and only testify to the critics' ignorance of the subject. We know that the Bank's system is not by any means a perfect one, but, surely, the person who advertises an infallible financial system is either a great rogue or a great simpleton; for why is he not himself rich beyond desire?

The Bank of England, it is admitted, cannot meet its liabilities on demand, and most people would think that its directors had gone mad if they prepared to, while the stockholders would certainly threaten to turn out those directors who proposed a policy which would reduce the value of their stock considerably below parity.

The question seems to be: Is the Bank of England sufficiently prepared to meet all likely withdrawals of gold by its customers and by the holders of its notes?

The two columns, which give us the amount of the Bank's liquid assets, tell us plainly enough that the Bank of England was well prepared on the 1st October. We can see that it held a good supply of coin and bullion, and, secondly, a valuable list of convertible securities; but as the securities are only convertible so long as the Bank, which holds the reserves of cash of all the banks in the United Kingdom, is in a position to meet all probable demands upon its store of gold, it is evident that the first ratio is of paramount importance.

The Bank of England, which possesses the only large store of the precious metals in this country, has to meet both the home and foreign demands for gold. It follows, therefore, that its ratio per cent. of Reserve to Liabilities is eagerly scrutinised each week on the publication of the return, because it indicates whether or not loanable capital is likely to be dear or cheap. The means at its disposal for maintaining an adequate supply in reserve will be discussed later on.

Should the said ratio fall below, say, forty per cent., then it is prudent to inquire the reason; and should it recede to, say, thirty-three or thirty-four per cent., then there may be cause even for apprehension; but so long as the Bank of England keeps a fair ratio of reserve to its public indebtedness, there is no cause for alarm: though a bank which holds the national reserve must always be extremely cautious, even when credit is good and there is not a breath of suspicion in the air, for the proverbial little cloud gathers strength with incredible speed when once it does appear.

Undoubtedly our banking system is exposed to the gravest dangers, but as it brings us cheap money we accept the risks; and unless a critic can produce a workable scheme which will eliminate the hazard and retain the blessing of cheap loanable capital, he had better by far confine his attention to those safeguards that reduce the risks of our present system, which *is* workable, to a minimum. Provided the Bank of England keeps an adequate reserve in the Banking Department, we have at least the satisfaction of knowing that all that can reasonably be done to ensure safety has been done, and that those risks, which a credit bank cannot avoid under any system, have at least been insured against under our own.

No doubt the Bank's large working capital of over £17,500,000 has contributed very considerably to its ascendancy, and helped it, especially since 1844, to more than hold its own against all comers; for despite the fact that we occasionally hear sneers—no doubt prompted by jealousy—at its so-styled omnipotence, an examination of its return soon convinces the sceptical that it is still the largest and safest bank in England. Further, it has occupied this enviable position for over two hundred years.

The ratio per cent. of Advances (loans, bills discounted, securities, &c.) to Liabilities is only 38·21—a proportion, especially when it is remembered that an unknown amount of investments is included therewith, which clearly informs us that the Bank is fully alive to the responsibilities of its unique position, and that its directors, while they are no doubt anxious to make as much net profit as possible for the proprietors, have not lost sight of the fact that they also have duties to perform towards the public.

But it must not be thought that the directors discharge their duties towards the public so well from philanthropic motives. Even from a selfish standpoint it pays them to keep the Bank thoroughly prepared, as, should they allow the reserve to sink too low, an anxious period would be certain to follow, when additional profits, made by trading with too large a proportion of the deposits, would speedily be swept away by the expense incurred by borrowing back at high rates in order to strengthen the cash in hand. For a little while the interest upon the increased loans would swell the profits, but directly the foreign exchanges moved against this country, and gold began to flow abroad, even an inexperienced director would realise the folly of risking a panic for the sake of seeing the dividends rise, and he would not make such a doubtful experiment a second time.

Perhaps, before bringing this chapter to a close, it may be interesting to compare the total indebtedness of the Bank of England to the public and its stockholders with that of Lloyds and the National Provincial Bank of England to their customers and shareholders. The following table will supply the figures:—

NAME OF BANK.	TOTAL LIABILITIES.
	£
Bank of England	101,681,010
Lloyds	58,411,041[*]
National Provincial Bank of England	56,444,126[*]

[*]Balance Sheet dated 31st December, 1901.

We can now see how much larger are the working resources of the Bank of England than those of either of the other above-mentioned banking institutions, though, as the joint stock banks keep their reserves of cash with the Bank of England, the comparison loses a little of its force. Still, the preponderance of the Bank of England is most marked, a fact one is not, perhaps, so apt to realise when the Issue and Banking Departments are considered apart.

CHAPTER V.
THE STORE IN THE ISSUE DEPARTMENT.

WE next have to consider the amount of gold coin and bullion in the Issue Department—to wit, £33,617,330, and we must remember that this accumulation is the national store, that the cash reserves of all the banks in England, Scotland, and Ireland are dependent thereupon, and that, consequently, the solvency of the nation is decided thereby.

The indebtedness of the English, Scotch, and Irish Banks to the public at December, 1901, as shown by their balance sheets, upon current accounts, deposit receipts, and notes in circulation, amounted to nearly £910,000,000. The liabilities of the Bank of England and of those private bankers who publish balance sheets are included in this huge total.

This £910,000,000 may be called the "floating capital" of the country. It is deposited or left with the banks, who invest a certain proportion of it in securities, in short loans to the bill brokers and stockbrokers, in making advances and loans to their customers, and in discounting bills for them; and, as the said millions are left at either call or short notice, the banks also have to maintain a sufficient supply of legal tender to meet all probable demands upon this immense debt. It is with this "floating capital" that the present chapter is principally concerned.

Stored in their strong rooms the banks keep sufficient legal tender (Bank of England notes and specie) with which to conduct their business. The sum thus held may be called their "till money"; and it probably would not exceed five per cent. of the £910,000,000 in question—viz.: £45,500,000. A large part of this till money is, however, held in Bank of England notes, which are warrants for gold upon the store in the Issue Department, but as creditors cannot refuse the notes they are quite as valuable to a banker as gold. All a banker has to consider is whether he has a sufficient supply of legal tender to discharge his public indebtedness; and if he have, he need take no thought for the morrow.

Deducting £45,500,000 from £910,000,000, we get £864,500,000. Though this is an accumulation of credit in the books of the banks rather than of cash, their customers can demand the equivalent from them in legal tender; yet we see that, were the banks drained of £45,500,000, they would then be entirely dependent upon their reserves at the Bank of England.

The reserves are included in Other Deposits, £42,695,526; and seeing the magnitude of the amount it seems a pity that the Bank of England does not tell us each week what portion of this total belongs to the other banks. Further, the Bank of England employs these balances in its own business; and, though it generally maintains a very large ratio per cent. of reserve to liabilities, the fact remains that a certain proportion of the cash reserves of our banks is lent out to the public—a somewhat startling position at first sight. The banks accumulate a reserve against those dangers from which their business is never free, and the Bank of England advances some of it to its own customers! Apparently, what could be more absurd? But in finance things are so often not what they seem.

We now come to the store of gold coin and bullion in the Issue Department—£33,617,330. A certain proportion of this must be retained in order to secure the convertibility of the notes of the Bank, and the remainder may perhaps be called the national store or accumulation. The banks of the United Kingdom are indebted, roughly speaking, to the public to the extent of £910,000,000. But we have seen that, say, £45,500,000 of this sum is secured by legal tender in hand, so the unsecured portion amounts to £864,500,000. Our position, then, stands as under:—

Indebtedness of the Banks of the United Kingdom to the public	£910,000,000
Less covered by legal tender (say)	45,500,000
	£864,500,000
Gold and bullion at the Bank of England	£35,800,000

As a matter of fact, we are looking on the bright side of the picture, for seeing that a large amount in Bank notes would be held among the £45,500,000 deducted, it follows that the store in the Issue Department might be appreciably reduced were a considerable number of these notes presented for payment; and then again, the indebtedness of those private bankers who do not publish balance sheets has been omitted. Suppose we say that the banks hold £35,500,000 in specie. This, added to the store at the Bank, gives us £71,300,000. Then our banks owe £910,000,000; but there is only £71,000,000 of specie in their possession with which to pay their huge debt. On the other hand, many of the banks do not hold nearly five per cent. of their liabilities to the public in legal tender on their premises; and, were the truth known, it is more than probable that in some instances three-and-a-half to four-and-a-half per cent. would be nearer the mark.

England, after all, is only a gigantic workshop, and so long as her shops are busy there is no danger. But have those people who live on incomes invested solely in British securities ever reflected that, were there no work for her shops, this system of credit would collapse like a castle of cards, when their incomes would be gone? Our solvency as a nation depends absolutely upon the skill and ability displayed by British manufacturers, and upon the muscles and intelligence of their workmen. Given a high standard of efficiency and adaptability on the part of our producers, then trade flows to this country, and by trade alone can we support our credit and pay our debts. Small wonder, then, that thoughtful people are becoming alarmed at the apotheosis of Games in this country, and at the large number of idlers who do not take a part in production, but are dependent upon the interest received from investments, which can only be productive so long as our commerce is flourishing.

The capital of this country has been computed by a competent authority at about £10,500,000,000, but doubtless these figures are very wide of the mark. Still, the amount of fixed capital invested in the country must be immense. By "fixed" capital, as distinguished from the floating or loanable capital deposited with the banks and kindred institutions, those investments of a more permanent character are implied. A depositor can demand his money back from his banker, but bank shares he would have to sell on the Stock Exchange—therefore the one is "floating" and the other "fixed" capital. It is the same with Consols, railway shares, and with the shares of all companies in which there is a market. When there is not a market, then the capital is fixed indeed; and there would not even be a market for Consols were the Bank of England drained of its gold. Moreover, during normal times the demand for loanable capital at the banks will help to determine the price an investor will receive should he desire to sell any of his fixed investments.

It consequently amounts to this: The fixed capital of the country cannot be converted or sold unless the banks maintain large cash reserves; so we may truthfully assert that about £10,000,000,000 of capital is erected on a basis of about £71,000,000 of cash. This cash, in its turn, can only be kept in the country while our workshops are busy; therefore it at once becomes apparent that the national aim should be to increase our trade, for the yield, and consequently the value, of British securities is bound to either increase or diminish in proportion as the trade of the country is either flourishing or the reverse. Even the Government can only meet the interest on Consols while the people are in a position to pay their taxes.

Such a statement may come as a shock to those persons who are accustomed to draw their dividends each half-year or year, and to imagine that unless the world came to an end these dividends could not cease; but they would cease were this country to fall hopelessly behind in the race for trade. This is not the old Socialist maxim that "Labour supports the world" put into a new print dress. It is evident that the fixed capital of this country, as represented by stocks and shares, would be mere waste paper unless the banks held sufficient gold to ensure a market for them: and as this gold cannot be kept in the country unless our workshops are able to compete successfully with those of other nations, it follows that the position of those persons who draw incomes from British securities is entirely dependent upon the brains and abilities of the men who direct our industries. How important, then, that the very best talent the nation possesses should be used in trade; and what folly it is on the part of those so-called "superior" persons to sneer at the trader—at him who, without doubt, enables them to draw their incomes regularly!

There was a time when capital, broadly speaking, could only be obtained in London; but since then population has increased all the world over, and as capital is only the savings of labour, it naturally follows that it can now be obtained abroad, and that London is less necessary to the foreign borrower; and, as the world fills up, it must surely become less and less necessary. Yet our gilded youth affects to despise trade. This is somewhat absurd, when it is trade that enables him to live in idleness; and British pride, unless it recognises this fact, may have a bad fall.

The banks of the United Kingdom, roughly speaking, are indebted to the public to the extent of £910,000,000. They only keep till-money in their safes, and are dependent upon the store in the Issue Department of the Bank of England for their reserves of cash. In other words, this £33,000,000 of specie is the foundation stone upon which £910,000,000 of credit rests. It has already been shown in what relation the fixed capital of the country stands to this fund.

The smaller of the provincial banking companies keep their cash reserves with their London agents, who also place their reserves with the Bank of England. Consequently, as the agents include the reserves of these banks with their own deposits, they, like the Bank of England in relation to the bankers' balances, lend out a percentage of the reserves of the smaller banks. It follows, therefore, that the bankers' balances in the hands of the Bank are smaller than would be the case if each bank kept its reserve with it. The London agents are dependent upon the Bank, and the smaller banks upon the agents.

As the store in the Issue Department is the only large collection of specie and bullion in the three kingdoms, and as the amount therein is always extremely small when compared with the huge liabilities which, under certain conditions, it might be asked to liquidate, any considerable depletion of this store makes the owners of large bank balances nervous; for if the Bank of England cannot pay the bankers, then their bankers will not be able to pay them.

Again, the liabilities of the banks are so immense in comparison with their reserves that a very small diminution of the fund in the Issue Department makes owners of capital anxious, whilst a serious drain would probably create a panic; and unless means were devised to allay the panic, it might develop into a revolution; for we are very commercial in these days, and are beginning to realise that mere glory may be bought too dearly. Commercialism, however, is not exactly a fascinating virtue.

We are constantly being told that the money market is an extremely sensitive organisation. And no wonder! The banks owe hundreds of millions on demand and short notice. Considerably over eighty per cent. of these millions is invested and lent, and as the banks' reserves of gold are small, every sudden demand for large supplies of the precious metals is liable to disorganise the market; and the Bank, which holds the final reserve, is therefore compelled to raise its rate of discount in order to protect the bullion in its Issue Department.

But for this very reason capital may generally be borrowed more cheaply in London than elsewhere; and though cash is perhaps dangerously economised, credit is proportionately the more easily obtainable, and the price of a loan is cheaper than would be the case were the banks to maintain a higher ratio of cash to liabilities. They would then have less to lend, and in times when trade was brisk demand would drive up the rate of interest to higher figures than those which prevail under our present system, and reduce the profits of borrowers. The average rate, too, would be greater.

The dangers of our system are very apparent, but so are its advantages; and though we consider it pays us to take the risks, it is evident that we cannot afford to neglect the necessary precautions.

CHAPTER VI.
WEEKLY DIFFERENCES IN THE RETURN.

IT were better, before proceeding further, to give a copy of the Bank Return as it appears in the daily papers each Friday, when comparisons are made with the figures of the preceding week, and the various differences carried into distinctive columns. That for the week ended Wednesday, 1st October, 1902, has been selected, in order that the figures may be the same throughout this volume. The statement is given below:

ISSUE DEPARTMENT.

2 OCT., 1901.		24 SEPT., 1902.	1 OCT., 1902.	INCREASE	DECREASE
£		£	£	£	£
36,080,595	Gold and Bullion	35,109,950	33,617,330	...	1,492,620
53,855,595	Notes Issued	53,284,950	51,792,330	...	1,492,620
30,546,875	Circulation	29,198,845	30,401,185	1,202,340	...

BANKING DEPARTMENT.

2 OCT., 1901.		24 SEPT., 1902.	1 OCT., 1902.	INCREASE.	DECREASE.
£	LIABILITIES.	£	£	£	£
3,790,617	Rest	3,804,611	3,816,736	12,125	...
10,874,58	Public	8,301,490	10,025,97	1,724,483	...

- 41 -

				Decrease	Increase
1	Deposits		3		
41,204,129	Other Deposits	40,373,382	42,695,526	2,322,144	...
143,965	Seven-Day Bills	192,886	188,590	...	4,296
£	ASSETS.	£	£	Decrease	Increase
18,022,103	Government Securities	14,594,260	15,826,080	...	1,231,820
27,158,440	Other Securities	26,302,606	31,837,516	...	5,534,910
23,308,720	Notes	24,086,105	21,391,145	2,694,960	...
2,077,029	Gold and Silver	2,242,398	2,225,084	17,314	...
				£6,771,026	£6,771,026
48⅝%	Ratio	53·87%	44·6%		
3%	Bank Rate	3%	4%		

===

Why, it may be asked, is so much importance attached to this return, and why do the critics, each week, endeavour to state precisely how much the "market" has borrowed from, or repaid to, the Bank, and to explain the cause of the various accretions and diminutions in the different assets and liabilities? With regard to the latter attempt, each critic, it is said, is quite convinced that he alone understands the true inwardness of the various movements which result in the increases and decreases recorded in our table; but it is just whispered that those persons at the Bank of England who *know* the cause laugh at their deductions.

The return is of the greatest moment to the public, for the simple reason that it shows the ratio per cent. of the Bank's reserve of notes and cash in hand to its liabilities, and, also, the amount of coin and bullion in the Issue Department. The Bank holds the final reserve; and if demand is brisk and the other bankers have advanced largely to the outside market, the bill brokers are driven to the Bank. As the banking companies have advanced all their spare capital, demand can only be supplied from the reserve at the Bank of England; and the Bank, which must protect its gold, checks demand by charging high rates to all who borrow.

The return, then, tells us whether loanable capital is likely to be cheap or dear. If the ratio to liabilities be small, and the store of gold diminishing, we know that demand has reached the Bank, and that money will be dear. When money is dear, Consols and other so-called gilt-edged securities are almost certain to fall in value. If it become really scarce, then the banks, which lend huge sums on the Stock Exchange, charge the brokers enhanced rates, and "carrying over" becomes difficult. Numerous speculative accounts have to be closed, and securities, consequently, fall in price.

Now, a glance at the return of 1st October, 1902, shows that the ratio on that date is 44·6 per cent., and the Bank's discount rate four per cent. The bullion in the Issue Department decreased £1,492,620, and the Bank, in order to arrest this drain, raised the rate from three to four per cent. The political unrest in France, which at first threatened to disturb the London money market, and the tightness of money in New York, were, undoubtedly, two factors which largely influenced the decision of the directors, who, no doubt, also took into their consideration the fact that the autumn demand for currency might further reduce their reserve. Noticing that Consols were at 93-1/8, and believing that the stringency was only temporary, one might feel disposed to buy, trusting that cheaper money during the earlier part of the new year would drive them up to 96 or so.

The weekly return of the Bank of England, then, is the barometer which tells us whether loanable capital is either scarce or abundant, dear or cheap; and, when read with the Board of Trade returns and the foreign exchanges, it enables us to guess, with more or less *uncertainty*, but still intelligently, and with a degree of probability, whether or not money is likely to be in future demand. The Railway and Bankers' Clearing House returns, too, indicate the course of trade, and are of more than academic interest. It is, however, always wise to remember that finance is not an exact science, for if it were the theorists would be fabulously rich; and we know that they are generally so hard up as to be compelled to write books and financial articles for a living.

Now we can see why the Bank of England's weekly balance sheet is keenly interesting to every person who possesses capital either to lend or to invest, to dealers in bills and securities, and to every speculator on the Stock Exchange, as a strong or a weak return may make all the difference to the rates charged on "contango" day. Borrowers and lenders are equally concerned, for the rate of interest does not depend upon the caprice of any individual or of any bank, but is solely the outcome or result of demand and supply; and demand, when the banks have exhausted their supplies of spare capital, then centres itself fiercely upon the Old Lady of Threadneedle Street simply because she holds the final reserve of cash, and for no other reason whatsoever.

Reverting to our statement, we find that the increases and decreases of the various totals balance each other; and if the differences agree, then the assets and liabilities, on adding the Bank's capital of £14,553,000 to the latter, must also balance each other, for the simple reason that the Bank keeps its books by double entry. The best system of bookkeeping which can possibly be adopted is the simplest system, because the very fact of accounts being complex and involved is sure to result in a multiplicity of mistakes, which prove that the system is faulty. In double entry there must be a debit for every credit; so every sum debited to one account in the books of the Bank of England is credited to another or to others; and as the assets and liabilities in the statement tally, therefore the balances in the last two columns, which are the result of multitudinous debits and credits made during the week, must agree also. But how is it possible for an outsider to follow these internal movements? He simply cannot. Consequently his deductions made from the differences shown week by week are sometimes very wide of the mark, and, for his own reputation's sake, it would be wiser if he were to confine his remarks principally to the all-important questions of the ratio in the Banking Department and the bullion in the Issue Department.

For instance, simply with the differences in question to go upon, it may be said that the return shows that the market has borrowed largely from the Bank, "Other Securities" being up over £5,000,000. Part of this amount increased "Other Deposits," and a transfer was also made to "Public Deposits" in order to pay the Government for £2,000,000 of Treasury bills, while the accretion to "Government Securities" seems to indicate that the Government borrowed a certain sum from the Bank on Ways and Means, and that loans were made to the market on this class of security.

In London the "loan account" system is greatly in evidence among the banks. That is to say, when a customer is granted a loan for, say, £10,000, his current account is credited £10,000, and a loan account, opened in his name, is debited £10,000. The interest is calculated upon the loan account, and the advantage resulting to the banks is too evident to call for explanation in these pages.

When loans are made by the Bank of England, accounts which increase "Other Securities" are debited, and other accounts, which increase "Other Deposits" are credited—if the loans are made to the public. Should the loans be made to the Government, "Public Deposits" and "Government Securities" also increase proportionately from the same cause. The Bank, because it keeps the bankers' accounts, occupies a peculiar position in relation to these entries, and that position will be discussed in a later chapter.

The notes in the Banking Department have decreased £2,694,960 and the specie £17,314, so, if we add these two sums together, the total, £2,712,274, represents the diminution in the reserve. A glance at the Bank's liabilities shows us that they have increased appreciably, and as the reserve has shrunk considerably, it follows that the ratio is very much smaller than that of the previous week. Indeed, the reserve had not fallen so low since May; and the monetary outlook being uncertain, the directors, as a precautionary measure, raised the rate of discount.

Next, suppose that we wish to ascertain the amount of cash which has been withdrawn from the Bank to meet the demand within the country. The bullion in the Issue Department is £1,492,620 down, and the coin in the Banking Department £17,314; so the Bank has lost £1,509,934 in coin and bullion. But £730,000 was exported during the week; therefore, if we deduct £730,000 from £1,509,934, the difference, £779,934, is the amount that is gone into home circulation.

But, it may be asked, how can one ascertain the amounts of the exports and imports of the precious metals? Late in the afternoon of each day the Bank exhibits a statement on its walls giving this information, and it was from these placards that it was ascertained that the sum in question had been sent abroad. Hence it is possible to learn how much cash was withdrawn from the Bank for home requirements during the week, or, better, the amount of the efflux on the day of the publication of the return.

But, as has already been explained, these deductions are not always reliable.

CHAPTER VII.
THE BANK OF ENGLAND AS AGENT OF THE MINT.

IN theory any person can take gold bullion to the Mint, which, under the Coinage Act, is compelled to give him in exchange sovereigns containing an equal quantity of gold to that left; but nobody ever does, and practically the Bank of England acts as the Mint's agent. By the Bank Act he receives £3 17s. 9d. per ounce, instead of £3 17s. 10-1/2d., the full Mint price, the deduction of 1-1/2d. being about equal to the loss of interest incurred, for the Mint does not bargain to pay out coin immediately on delivery of bullion.

All the bankers in the United Kingdom, we know, obtain their supplies of cash from the Issue Department of the Bank of England, which, as a natural consequence, supplies the currency requirements of the nation. Possessing the only large store of bullion, it can, so to speak, feel the pulse of the whole trading community; and, directly a demand sets in for specie, it sends bullion to the Mint for conversion into coin. This it can do without any loss of interest whatever, for, of course, the bullion is lying idle in the Issue Department. A bank which keeps the Government accounts, and stands in this relation to the other bankers, must of necessity become the agent of the Mint, which, even in its output of silver and bronze coins, relies absolutely upon information received from the Bank of England. The Bank, in fact, supplies both the London and country bankers with these token coins.

As an illustration of this one of those little social amenities which take place between bankers and their clients about Christmas time may be mentioned. Naturally I am not alluding to the higgling occasioned by the increase of advances and bills discounted to meet a growing demand at this period of the year. But many persons, just before the festive season sets in, like to obtain supplies of bright new silver coins with which to anoint the palms of their humbler fellow-subjects, whose manners about that time become aggressively pleasant and ingratiating. These coins they get from their bankers, who receive them from the Bank of England and its branches, either directly or through their agents. As soon as the bankers run short of silver coins, they apply to the Bank, which, being in close touch with every source of demand, is able to guide the Mint on a question of supply.

The Bank of England does not possess a legal monopoly, but occupies this position solely because it holds the final reserve of cash. If the Government and all the bankers keep accounts with the Bank of England, then the Bank must act as the agent of the Mint so long as this state of affairs continues, because its Issue Department has to meet all demands for cash made upon it by the Bank's customers and the holders of its notes; and as these customers, either directly or indirectly, include every large dealer in gold in the land, it supplies the currency as a matter of course. Dealers do not send their bullion to the Mint, because it is more convenient to sell it outright to the Bank, which settles with them immediately, thereby removing all uncertainty as to the length of time coinage will occupy.

It follows, therefore, that the Bank of England has to meet all demands for gold, whether for home or foreign requirement; but it is when gold is leaving the country in large quantities that drastic measures have to be taken in order to stop the depletion of the Bank's reserve of the precious metals, for some of the home drains are only of a temporary nature, and unless capital be greatly in demand at the time they do not affect the rate of interest, as the money flows back to the Bank after a short interval.

The Bank of England on 5th January, 5th April, 5th July, and 5th October pays the quarterly dividends on the National Debt. The Government, which at the present time has to provide over £6,000,000 each quarter, has a huge sum standing to its credit before one of these payments matures, and the sudden release of so much capital often causes the rate of discount to fall, especially during those years when trade is good, and the demand for loanable capital consequently brisk. If times are dull, then the rate will not ascend when the Government is taking money off the market, as the demand upon the reduced resources of the banks will not be sufficiently keen to drive a large number of borrowers to the Bank of England.

We have an illustration of this in the fact that from February, 1894, to September, 1896, trade was so inactive, and demand therefore so small, that the Bank rate stood at two per cent. during the whole period. In other words, we had two and a half years with the Bank rate at two per cent. With trade bad and money cheap, speculation soon became rampant. The gilt-edged variety of securities yielded less, because trade was less productive, and consequently capital, instead of being kept idle in the banks, was transferred to the better class securities, which returned less to the investor in proportion as increased demand forced up prices. With incomes reduced and balances lying idle at the banks, the public developed a speculative mania, and one result was the Stock Exchange boom of 1895, for investment business and speculation always increase when trade is bad. Bad times, in fact, at first add to the business of the House.

Traders keep large balances with the banks for the same reason that the banks themselves have huge sums standing to their credit in the books of the Bank of England, because they are bound to accumulate credit in order to meet their engagements, and, also, to maintain a surplus in case of accidents, such as bad debts and the inability of customers to pay their debts immediately on maturity. When trade slackens and prices fall, producers reduce their output, and the result is an accumulation of credit in the books of the banks. Moreover, a certain proportion of these balances is not then required to finance and guarantee commercial undertakings. Hence the movement to which attention has already been drawn.

But the holders of gilt-edged securities require some inducement in order to persuade them to sell; and this is forthcoming in the shape of accretions to the capital value of their stocks and shares as a result of the increased demand. But the floating capital of the country is not decreased by this exchange. It is left at precisely the same figures. The buyers draw cheques upon their bankers, and the sellers pay the same cheques to their own credit; consequently, the floating capital in the hands of the banks is always about the same, be the times good or bad, so long as speculation or investment is confined to British securities. When, however, foreign securities are purchased, gold sometimes has to be sent out of the country to help pay for them; and it is then that the situation may cause apprehension—for capital is leaving the country. Should the drain prove serious, the Bank would have to raise its rate; and were it to prove continuous, notwithstanding an abnormally high Bank rate, we might have a crisis.

Returning to the dividends on the funds, "Public Deposits" are increased before the above-mentioned dates, and when this money is released, the result is a large addition to "Other Deposits," because most of the money returns to increase the bankers' balances. A small part, however, is taken by the fund-holders in cash; so we may notice a decrease in the Bank's reserve of notes, and, consequently, an increase in the circulation, together, perhaps, with a fall in the bullion, representing the small proportion withdrawn in actual cash. Should the banks, in consequence of this increase in their deposits, be taking bills from the brokers at cheaper rates, then "Other Securities" would also lessen, because the bill brokers would pay off the Bank and borrow in the cheaper market. The converse occurs when the Government is collecting the revenue, issuing a new loan, or borrowing on Treasury bills.

The principal currency drains will be discussed in the following chapter.

CHAPTER VIII.
THE PRINCIPAL CURRENCY DRAINS.

THE principal currency drains occur during the holiday season and at harvest time, more especially during the latter period, when large amounts of cash are sent into the country to satisfy the requirements of labour. Early in November a demand for gold arises in Scotland, owing to the fact that rents there fall due at Martinmas (11th November); and as the Scotch banks, by the Act of 1845, are compelled to hold gold against notes circulated in excess of their authorised issues, a rather heavy call is made upon the Bank of England, whose returns then show a noticeable decrease in the reserve and bullion. During years of active trade, and, consequently, of brisk demand for loanable capital, these autumnal drains of gold generally force up the rate of interest, thereby making the last quarter of the year the dearest for borrowers.

But we are discussing internal demands only, and as, so long as gold does not leave the country, it is merely a question of certain sums flowing from the London money market and drifting back to it again, this ebb and flow, which is shown by the various ups and downs occurring from time to time in the items of the Bank return, does not create any apprehension. Indeed, these movements occur so regularly at certain times of the year that large borrowers often anticipate them in order that they may tide over such periods with the minimum of inconvenience. It is, however, otherwise when gold is leaving the country in large quantities in order to settle the balance of our indebtedness to other nations, for that *may* not come back. How it is again enticed to these shores I will endeavour to explain.

We now come to a foreign drain of gold; and this depletion of the currency, we know, flows from the store at the Bank of England into the hands of the foreign creditors of the nation. We export to, and import from, other nations on a gigantic scale, and as our imports are invariably in excess of our exports, it follows that the balance of indebtedness on this score is always very considerably against us; but there are other debts due to this country which from time to time turn the balance in favour of England, and the prices quoted for bills on the various Exchanges are the indexes which tell us whether gold is likely to be either received from, or sent to, the great commercial centres of the world.

Other debts due to this country have been mentioned—debts which either tend to reduce or turn in our favour the balance we owe to foreign countries. England has immense sums invested in foreign securities, and the interest received therefrom acts in this direction. So, too, does the huge sum earned by her ships in the shape of freights. Then, again, London, still earns a large amount in the shape of commissions, even if her position as the Clearing House of the world is now less powerful than formerly, owing to large accumulations of capital in other centres.

On the other hand a considerable amount of foreign capital is invested in English securities, which, when sold on the Stock Exchange, give the foreigner a claim on our stock of gold; and though we, by similar sales of foreign securities, can prevent this temporary drain of specie, the enormous dealings in stocks and shares on the various Exchanges are most keenly watched by the directors of the Bank of England, lest huge realisations of British securities by foreigners should drain the Bank of its gold, with which international indebtedness can alone be settled.

This brings us to the markets for bills of exchange, the prices of which, like those of every other security, are settled by supply and demand. If, at a given date, this country owes a foreign nation considerably more than it has to receive, then bills on England will be plentiful in that country; and, further, they will be cheap, because, as debtors to England have less to remit than the aggregate of bills on England offered for sale, the supply will be in excess of the demand, and English bills, consequently, can be bought at a discount. Conversely, the supply of bills in London on the foreign country will be smaller than the sum English debtors owe therein, and in order to save the expense of exporting gold, such bills will be eagerly sought after, and, as the supply is smaller than the demand, buyers soon drive them to a premium, when the rate of exchange is said to be "unfavourable" to England.

As the balance of our international indebtedness must be cancelled by gold, it follows that the fewer the bills offering the higher will be the prices paid for them; and when, just towards the end, it becomes evident that the supply is limited the bidding is often spirited; but the premium paid cannot exceed for any considerable length of time the expense incurred by exporting and insuring the precious metals between any two countries, as the debtor always has the choice of despatching gold to his foreign creditor, and, naturally, he chooses the cheaper expedient.

The extreme fluctuations are called "gold points," and they mark the limit to premiums procurable on bills of exchange. The table given below will show us those points at which gold will probably either leave or reach this country:

EXCHANGE.	MINT PAR. OF EXCHANGE.	GOLD EXPORTS.	GOLD IMPORTS.
London on Paris	Francs 25·22½	25·12½	25·32½
Berlin	Marks 20·43	20·34	20·52
New York	Dollars 4·87	4·84	4·90

When the rates are near those given in the second column, the Bank, if its reserve be low, begins to consider the advisability of raising its rate of discount, for it is evident that foreign bills are at a stiff premium, and that a demand for gold may be made upon it at any moment. Of course the difference between the "gold points" gives scope for speculation, and some cambists gamble in bills for the rise or the fall just as speculators do in securities. Then, again, the arbitrageurs largely influence prices by buying and selling securities which are dealt in on the Stock Exchanges of more than one country. Wars, revolutions, panics, and social upheavals also cause abnormal fluctuations in the rates.

Let us assume that a drain is threatened from Paris. The gold in an English sovereign is, we can see, worth about 25·22½ francs, and if only 25·12½ is being offered on 'Change, it follows that bullion will soon be exported to France. This the Bank wants to prevent. The cost of transmission of bullion between the two countries is about one half per cent.; therefore, in order to induce French capitalists to invest in English bills of three months' date, the rate of interest in London must be more than two per cent. in excess of that in Paris before it will pay them to ship bullion to this country, if it be the intention of the purchasers to withdraw their capital when the bills mature, as the gain of two per cent. per annum for three months only just balances the loss of 10s. per cent. incurred on specie shipments, while no margin is left to defray possible loss through unfavourable exchanges at the time of withdrawal. Were a purchase of six months' bills contemplated, the difference in the two rates would only have to exceed one per cent. before bullion could be exported profitably.

When, therefore, the Bank of England wishes to influence the foreign exchanges, it raises its rate by one, instead of by one half as is usual when the drain is caused by the currency requirements of this country, or by an increased demand for loanable capital when trade is active and the foreign exchanges favourable. One constantly hears the question: Why has the Bank of England raised the rate by one instead of by one half as it did last time? A glance at the foreign exchange tables will generally supply the answer. If the expenses for transporting and insuring bullion between any two countries are appreciable, then were the Bank rate raised by one half (remembering that an addition of one half per cent. per annum gives a profit of only 2s. 6d. per cent. on a transaction in three months' bills) it is evident that the inducement is not sufficient to attract gold over here for that consideration alone.

By raising its rate, and, if necessary, borrowing in the market in order to bring the market rates in touch with its own, the Bank makes an investment in English bills a profitable transaction; and the greater its excess over foreign rates, the stronger is the inducement to send money to England. Of course, were this country really living on its capital, this influx of gold would only postpone the inevitable day of settlement, for a bankrupt does not increase his wealth by borrowing from one person in order to pay off another. But our receipts do not always coincide with our payments; and when, for instance, gold is sent to the United States in the autumn to help to pay for crops imported here, the Bank of England, by raising its rate of discount, and making that rate a representative one, attracts gold from the Continent, in order to tide over the interval between debts payable by us immediately and debts due to us at a future date.

English bills being a profitable investment, the price of paper on England at once begins to rise, and when the so-called gold point is reached the precious metals are shipped to these shores, because the premium on bills on England is in excess of the cost of despatching bullion. Every rise in the rate of discount here induces foreign holders of long-dated paper on England to retain their purchases. If they bought three months' bills on England when the Bank's discount rate was three, interest at the rate of three per cent. per annum was deducted from the face value of the bill to make it equivalent to a bill due at sight. Should the minimum rate be raised to four per cent., and were the holders then to remit the bills to this country to be discounted, they would have to submit to a deduction at the rate of four per cent. per annum. In other words, they would lose one per cent. per annum on the transaction. Long-dated bills would therefore be held until near maturity in order to avoid this loss.

An accretion to the Bank rate, then, not only attracts gold or capital here, but it also induces foreign holders of long-dated bills on England to keep them in their cases. On the other hand, a fall in the Bank's rate of discount from, say, three to two per cent. might not only slacken the demand for

English bills, but it would also cause a considerable number of long-dated bills on England to be sent over here to be discounted, as the foreign holders would naturally be anxious to secure the profit between the three per cent. per annum paid to them, and the two per cent. per annum at which they would then be taken from them. The result might possibly be a temporary drain of gold from this side.

But it is when a home and a foreign efflux of gold occur at the same time that the situation becomes serious, and unless immediate action is taken by the directors of the Bank of England to check the outflow, there is always the danger—so small is our gold reserve when contrasted with our exports and imports—that a balance against us at an unlucky moment may create an awkward tension, which, unless speedily relieved, may possibly produce a crisis.

We like to flatter ourselves that England is always safe; but so large is the amount of bills offering from day to day in the London money market that the very doubt of there not being sufficient capital in the possession of the banks to discount them creates uneasiness; and if it were thought that the Bank of England, which holds the few millions of reserve upon which hundreds of millions of credit rest, could not retain its gold, excitement would reach fever pitch in this country, for everybody's income would be in danger, and the Government, whose supineness allowed such a state of affairs to develop, would be in danger too. But we know that, in the rate of discount, the directors of the Bank possess an effective instrument to prevent such a catastrophe, and have the experience to use it to advantage.

Money begins to leave the Bank for internal circulation during the summer months in order to meet the demands created by the holidays and the harvest, and then in October there is always the probability of a large outflow of gold to the States to help pay for the crops imported therefrom; while the movement of specie to Scotland in November, occurring as it does just at a critical moment, is likely to cause some apprehension, should the Bank's reserve have been depleted earlier, unless the fact that it is merely a temporary transfer to enable the Scotch banks to comply with the Act of 1845 be thoroughly grasped.

The October drain of gold from the Bank when the New York exchange is unfavourable has in it an element of danger, especially if it happen at a time when the reserve at the Bank of England is unusually low; and if loanable capital be then abnormally scarce there is always the risk that the end of the year requirements may produce a tension, which, should credit be bad at the time, may develop into a panic.

If the Bank manage well, however, it fortunately often foresees that the autumnal demands may possibly impose a severe temporary strain upon its resources, and by raising its rate in anticipation of a short period of exceptional demand, it attracts gold to itself in order to be thoroughly prepared for possible large depletions of currency later on, for it is easier to accumulate gold before the event than to check an outflow when the movement is beginning to create uneasiness, and to attract attention to the lack of preparedness on the part of the Bank to meet large withdrawals of specie for export.

It is not my intention to write a treatise on the foreign exchanges, and I am quite well aware that I have only touched on the fringe of a great subject; but if these illustrations help, however slightly, to elucidate certain of those undercurrents which determine prices, then the sole aim of this chapter has been attained.

CHAPTER IX.
BANKS AND THE CREATION OF CREDIT.

WE have seen how the Bank of England came to occupy so commanding a position in the money market, and we now have to consider why its rate of discount is still a fairly reliable index to the value of loanable capital. Its advent was extremely distasteful to the private bankers, who then reigned supreme in London, and who were not slow to recognise in the new corporation a formidable competitor, for a company which financed the Government was obviously to be feared. Before 1826 the Bank of England was the only joint stock bank in the country. Its notes gradually drove those of the London bankers out of circulation, and until its joint stock rivals firmly established themselves in the Metropolis, the Bank was in every sense the most powerful institution of its kind in the land.

Being by far the largest lender of capital in the country, it was only natural that its rate should accurately interpret those forces which make loanable capital dear or cheap, as the case may be. But the Bank could not arbitrarily fix the value of money for a very considerable period, even when it was able to issue notes without let or hindrance, any more than it can now. Supply and demand must settle that ultimately; and whenever the Bank inflated prices by the over-issue of paper, we have seen that the reaction produced thereby invariably threatened its existence. This is easily explained.

Persons borrow money in order that they may trade with it; and sudden loans of large amounts of capital in the shape of notes immediately stimulate the markets, and the increased demand engendered thereby causes the prices of commodities to rise. Rising prices, whether of securities or goods, give a marked impetus to speculation—so hopeful are traders directly markets begin to improve; and increased speculation causes further rises in the prices of both commodities and loanable capital. Everybody wants to borrow, and to share, in the coming period of great prosperity.

With prices rising here, imports naturally increase, as foreigners are anxious to sell their goods in the best market. On the other hand, the English markets have become less profitable to buyers, and, consequently, exports fall off, the result being that the balance of our indebtedness to other nations is largely increased. The foreign exchanges soon begin to move against England, and the Bank of England (we will assume) which had created the speculation by large issues of notes, suddenly finds that it is threatened with a foreign drain of gold, and is compelled to raise its rate in order to protect its reserve.

Since 1844 this power has, of course, been taken out of the hands of the Bank; but it is evident that, even before that date, the Bank of England could not fix the rate of discount, for whenever it made the attempt it failed signally. The above illustration fully explains the reason why. Both before and after the Act the Bank of England would have suspended payment upon more than one occasion, when it neglected to keep an adequate reserve, but for Government intervention; and it will be in the same plight again if it trade with too large a proportion of its resources.

The Bank was then by far the largest dealer in credit, and from time to time it stated the minimum rate at which it would lend or discount. But the private bankers were at liberty to underbid it; and although it could, by making sudden advances, cause money to fall in value, its power was not of a lasting character, and the rise which followed was quite beyond its control. Its rivals are now much more powerful, and the Bank is only one large dealer among many—therefore it has to either raise or lower its rate according to the demands made upon its resources; but from its position in the centre of the money market it still possesses a latent power for possible evil, which appears to have escaped the attention it deserves.

This brings us to the vexed question of the creation of credit by a bank, and though it is stoutly maintained that an ordinary banking company cannot create credit, I venture to think that, given certain conditions, it does. But perhaps, before proceeding further, it will be better to briefly discuss the Clearing House system.

Cheques and bills, we all know, pour up to London in a constant stream to the numerous banks, and are presented by them either to the firms upon whom they are drawn or to their agents at the Lombard Street Clearing House. As every bank which is a member of the Clearing House keeps an account with the Bank of England, the debit and credit balances (the result of this exchange) are adjusted in the books of the Bank at the end of each day, and so, though the balances standing to the credit of the various banks are diminished or increased, the total sum to the credit of all the clearing bankers remains unaltered. In other words, the balances, which are the outcome of the exchange of credit documents at the Clearing House, are finally arranged by transfer entries in the books of the Bank of England.

Every cheque presented in the House is debited to one bank and credited by another, therefore the totals of the debit and credit entries must agree; and if the totals are the same, then the debit and credit balances must agree also. In the smaller towns the banks exchange the local cheques between themselves, and settle the balances in cash or by payments through

London. But Birmingham, Bristol, Leeds, Leicester, Liverpool, Manchester, and Newcastle-on-Tyne have Clearing Houses of their own at which local cheques and bills are presented.

We can now approach the question of the creation of credit by a bank. Suppose a bank suddenly increases its advances to its customers by £1,000,000, and that the customers pay away the whole sum by cheques. The said cheques are, say, paid by the recipients to the credit of their accounts with other banks, which present them at the London Clearing House. The balance of the bank which made the advance is thereby reduced £1,000,000 at the Bank, and the accounts of other banks are credited to the same extent; so the deposits at the Bank of England are not reduced one penny by the transfer. But £1,000,000 has been added to the working resources of the other banks; and as the liabilities of the bank that made the advance have not been reduced, surely this is a creation of credit? Of course, the bank which made the loan has lost £1,000,000 in "cash" at the Bank of England, and that asset would then be merged in "advances," which are up £1,000,000; and though the bank has not created credit in its own books, it has in those of its rivals. Surely, then, every bank which makes a new advance to a customer, who employs the sum placed to his credit to cancel certain debts of his own, creates credit in the books of other institutions. But the Bank of England can also create credit in its own.

On the other hand, say, Bank A calls in £1,000,000 from the bill brokers, who obtain credit to the extent of £1,000,000 from, say, Bank C, and draw cheques thereupon, and hand them to Bank A, which takes them to the Clearing House. C's balance at the Bank is reduced by £1,000,000, and A's is increased by a like sum; but in neither case is the "liabilities" side of the balance sheet affected. It is a mere transfer of credit from one account on the "assets" side to another on the same side, while the bankers' balances at the Bank of England remain the same. However, should Bank A advance £1,000,000 to a customer, who draws cheques against it, then the creation of credit in the books of other banks begins, as illustrated by our first example.

Again, take the case of a bank which sells securities, say Consols, to the amount of £1,000,000. It receives cheques upon other banks for a like sum; and these it takes to the Clearing House, where it presents them to those banks upon which they are drawn. The result is that the selling bank's balance at the Bank is up £1,000,000, and that the accounts of the other banks are down £1,000,000; but their liabilities also are down £1,000,000, whereas the liabilities of the selling bank are precisely the same. It has simply transferred £1,000,000 from Consols to "cash" at the Bank of England on the "assets" side of its balance sheet. Such a sale has reduced the floating capital of the banks by £1,000,000. Further, could not a little "window dressing" be done in this manner were a bank to find itself short of "cash" at the end of the half-year? By lending the sum so obtained the selling bank could create an amount of credit in the books of its rivals similar to that which it had previously destroyed. By buying stock back, too, it would produce exactly the same effect as if it made a loan.

Now we come to the creation of credit by the Bank of England in its own books. Were the Bank to suddenly lend £3,000,000, the "Other Deposits" would be up to that extent, and "Other Securities" would also be up to a like amount, because the Bank would credit its customers and debit the loans. Both sides of its return are increased, but, so far, credit has not been created by these mere book entries, though the way for its creation has been prepared. The customers or persons to whom the advances have been made begin to draw upon their accounts by cheques, and as these cheques are returned by the other bankers to the credit of their accounts (bankers' balances) it follows that "Other Deposits" are not reduced at the Bank. The Bank, then, has created £3,000,000 of credit in its books, and though it can no longer make sudden loans by a huge issue of notes as was possible prior to 1844, yet, because it holds the bankers' balances, we can see that it is able to produce precisely the same effect by means of another instrument.

If the Bank lends £3,000,000 to the Government, "Public Deposits" and "Government Securities" advance proportionately. When the Government begins to pay out, then a large part of this sum returns to "Bankers' Balances," and credit is created at the Bank of England to the extent of the sum so returned. But the banks (Lombard Street) have more to lend; therefore money is made artificially cheap.

On the other hand, the Government sometimes borrows in the open market on Treasury bills. Credit is then transferred at the Bank through the medium of the Clearing House from "Bankers' Balances" to "Public Deposits." The resources of Lombard Street are reduced, and until Government disbursements are made, and credit thereby transferred to Lombard Street, money becomes tight, and borrowers are often driven to the Bank.

We have seen that in the end an over-issue of notes is certain to reduce the Bank's reserve to a dangerously low level, and that, therefore, directors who know their business would hesitate to make so risky an experiment. The same argument is equally applicable to the creation of credit by sudden large loans on the part of the Bank in its own books. Such loans, we have seen, increase both sides of the return; but the Bank's reserve of notes and coin in the Banking Department remains at the same figures, consequently, its ratio per cent. to liabilities shows an ominous decline, which is, of itself, a warning that something is wrong.

Let us assume that the Bank suddenly lends £5,000,000. Money is thereby made artificially cheap, and the market rate for bills must fall in consequence. But the bankers' balances have been increased in the books of the Bank of England, and Lombard Street is not going to quietly look on while Threadneedle Street does all the business. Consequently, the bankers lend a portion of their balances at lower rates still, in order to attract business to themselves, and the market rate falls again. Here we have a situation analogous to that described in the earlier part of this chapter.

Now suppose this movement took place in October, and that a drain of gold occurred outwards. The Bank, in order to arrest the said drain, would have to raise its rate, and to bring the market rate in touch with its own it would be compelled to sell Consols, thereby reducing the bankers' balances in its books, and, of course, lessening the power of the banks to lend. But such a process is an expensive one, for the Bank is in reality borrowing back at panic prices the capital it created during a time of temporary ease.

Although the Bank undoubtedly possesses this power, the directors are not likely to abuse it, because the risk incurred is out of all proportion to the possible gain if the deal is carried through successfully; so we may say that their power to create credit in their books is limited or regulated by the ratio per cent. of the Bank's reserve to its liabilities.

Of course, it may be asked: Is it safe to entrust such power to a board of directors who have to earn dividends for a body of stockholders?

That is a difficult question to answer, and one, moreover, to which there is no occasion to reply in this work. It may safely be said that no director who understands his business would take the risk upon any consideration; but there is the remote chance that an incompetent Governor might be placed at the helm, and in that event, however improbable, should he lose sight of everything but the dividends, he might create a terrible panic throughout the land. On the other hand, all who see the Bank return from week to week may read the signs, and should the ratio fall abnormally low the critics would flagellate the Governor unmercifully, and the business man, who is unaccustomed to the pleasantries of criticism, unless he be a most hardened member of his species, squirms under such a lash, fearful that his friends may read just what the Press thinks of him; so he takes heed.

Though the Bank's rate is not always the same as the market rate, it is seldom very much out of touch therewith. When the directors find that their rate of discount is too high to attract custom, then, if the reserve be also high, they lower their minimum in order to get a fair share of the business that is doing. Their other alternative, of course, is to borrow on stock, and in that manner to compel the bill brokers to pay them a reluctant visit.

The policy of the Bank has never been one of "grab," though the bill brokers often grumble; but its position, in relation to the market, is an extremely difficult one, so difficult at times as to be fraught with great anxiety; and remembering the power that devolves upon it by reason of its holding the bankers' balances, its policy seems one of enviable restraint and moderation. But that is only what everybody expects of the Bank of England.

CHAPTER X.
THE BATTLE OF THE BANKS.

BUT little has hitherto been said concerning the relations of the Bank of England with its rivals in the money market, and in order to trace the movement from its beginning we must return to 1826, in which year joint stock banks could be established in England at a greater distance than sixty-five miles from London. The Bank stoutly resisted this innovation, but the Government, in consequence of the constant failures of the country private bankers, passed the Act of 1826, and the thin edge of the wedge once inserted, the Bank's monopoly in London soon disappeared.

The London and Westminster, despite the determined opposition of the Bank of England, opened business in London during 1834, and the Bank's monopoly of banking was gone. All that then remained to it was the exclusive privilege of issuing notes in and within sixty-five miles of London, the only legal monopoly it still enjoys. Unable to keep the joint stock banks out of London the Bank actively opposed them, as also did the private bankers, who, while the Bank refused to open accounts for the new companies in its books, declined to admit them into the Clearing House, which was founded by the London bankers about 1775. The irony of Fate! They are now a feeble minority in a house of their own building. But history—both domestic and economic—can supply parallel instances.

Although the new system was destined to drive out the old, the joint stock banks made a bad start, and failures were at first so frequent that the public began to share the opinion of the Bank and to look upon them as anything but safe institutions. They were born in disaster, and their policy did not provide an antidote to the old evils; but, like the Bank of England itself, they were taught prudence by a series of panics and upheavals which threatened to wipe them out of existence. They were, in short, licked into shape, and that cautious prudent policy which now distinguishes our great banking companies is the fruit of a very bitter experience.

Towards the middle of the nineteenth century the manufactures of Great Britain began to increase by leaps and bounds, and population, which always augments rapidly when food is cheap and abundant, kept pace with the country's unprecedented commercial activity. In 1801 the population of London was less than one million. In 1837 it had increased to about two millions; and at the present time Greater London contains over six and a half millions.

It is quite evident that the Bank of England could not alone minister to the increasing wants of London, and both in the Metropolis and in the provinces its joint stock rivals rapidly accumulated credit. In June, 1854, the new banks were admitted into the Clearing House, and since that date they have carried all before them. They shared in the almost magical increase in the volume of British trade, but they neither created nor provided the incentive to that remarkable outburst of national prosperity which was the result of Free Trade, and which made this country the workshop of the world. Since then, however, the world has filled up.

The population of the United States in 1870 was 38,500,000; in 1900, 75,500,000. In 1871 the population of the German Empire was 41,000,000. In 1901 it had increased to 56,000,000. During the same period the population of the United Kingdom increased from 31,500,000 to 41,500,000. There are more people in the world to be fed, and as the earth fills up the struggle for existence must surely become fiercer. Noticing this, people naturally inquire whether, seeing the changed environment, Free Trade is suitable to the times. Some years ago, when trade was bad, the bimetallic controversy was raging, but since 1895 its advocates have been dumb, for the simple reason that people will not listen to theorists when times are good. They are then too intent upon making money. They think they may not get the chance again.

No doubt, when the depressed portion of the cycle came round bimetallists would have been heard again. But in the place of Bimetallism we now find Protection, and, in all truth, the question is serious enough; for, when the present wave of prosperity dies out in the States, there seems every probability that the huge American trusts will endeavour to swamp our markets with their goods. Free traders make quite a profession of faith of their commercial opinion. They declare that they are free traders with the same fervour they might infuse into the avowal that they were Protestants or Roman Catholics. But modern Christianity is eminently adaptable to every fresh situation. Is Free Trade?

The worse the times become, the louder, probably, will grow the controversy between the free traders and the protectionists; and when we remember that our workshops support our credit, and upon what an amazingly small reserve of the precious metals that credit is based, it is evident that the question ought to be approached with the greatest caution; for a decision that emptied our workshops would ruin the nation.

As the savings of the country increased, the joint stock banks accumulated credit with astonishing rapidity, and the Bank of England, slow to recognise the power of the new system, which was so admirably suited to the changed environment, was compelled to receive its hated rivals into the fold. The companies possessed no vaults for the storage of the precious metals on a large scale, and they were therefore glad to avail themselves of the facilities at the disposal of the Bank, whose premises were much better protected than their own. And then, again, as the Bank's notes were legal tender, the companies could send them from the head offices to the branches cheaply, while they were a convenient form in which to keep a certain proportion of their cash in hand.

The evolution of the Bank of England, we can see, has not proceeded smoothly; but it is remarkable that an institution, which owed its pre-eminence entirely to monopoly, did not gradually begin to sink into a second-rate banking company directly its exclusive privilege of joint stock banking was abrogated and free trade in banking established in England. So conservative was the Bank's policy that it seems little short of marvellous that its joint stock rivals should have quietly endured its studied insults. The new movement was then, however, not only in its infancy, but was under a cloud as well, and through the companies grouping themselves around the Bank they enabled that institution to retain its position in the centre of the money market. The power incident to that position has been fully explained in the previous chapter.

The London private bankers, whose lack of enterprise can only be attributed to the fact that they were imbued with those narrow City traditions which make London the home of Conservatism, also quite failed to grasp the situation, and allowed the new companies to expand in every direction, confident that so sudden a change must end in disaster, and, therefore, they were content to look on, to shake their heads sadly at the unprofessional conduct of those new banks, and to soothe their feelings by ever and anon declaring, with due solemnity, that joint stock banking would ruin the country.

Certainly, the new companies did not manage well at first, and a few of them were wiped out in consequence; but, in spite of mistakes, they progressed, because their system was adaptable to the requirements of a growing England. In these times it is the fashion to apotheosise man—to picture him as a kind of demi-god; therefore, it is asserted that man makes his mark on the times. But it is surely more rational and logical to assume that the times gradually mould the particular cast of brain that is adaptable to a constantly changing environment, and that the man who chances to possess that cast of brain goes with the tide—which takes him a long way. At any rate, such was the case with the joint stock banks, which owe their success entirely to the adaptability of their system to a changing market. Moreover, that market is still changing.

The old-fashioned London bankers found, to their great surprise, that they had not read the signs of the times aright; but the orthodox seldom play the *rôle* of a prophet successfully, because they have lived too long in one groove, and so are apt to forget that England is not the world, which is steadily increasing in population. Instead of failing, the joint stock banks merely occupied the ground, and, by so doing, confined the business of the London private banker to the one street in which he was established and in which his father lived before him. They had no respect for age—those new companies!

The joint stock banks spread their tentacles north, south, east, and west of his sacred City, thereby effectually preventing his expansion, and "concentrating" his energies in the one street aforesaid, just as the nations of Europe have "concentrated" the kingdom of the unspeakable Turk. Great movements seldom originate within London, which is strikingly lacking in originality, and that new blood from the provinces which flows in an ever-increasing stream towards the great City, and alone arrests decay, also seems to bring with it the new ideas.

The London private bankers waited in vain for the expected disappearance of their rivals, who, despite severe panics and crises, continued to add rapidly to their resources, until, surrounded by rival branches, profitable expansion became difficult for the private banker, whose business is now so localised as to render effective competition with the companies impossible. He cannot make rapid progress because he does not possess the branches through which alone the necessary credit can flow to the central office, and therefore the extinction of private banking in its present form seems only a question of time, for the wealthy are certain to deal with those banks whose vast accumulations are at least the outward and visible sign of the confidence the public has in their stability.

But the joint stock banks did not confine their energies to London. The London and South Western Bank, which was established in 1862, began a vigorous crusade in the London suburbs, with the happiest results to its shareholders; and the London and Provincial Bank, which was formed two years later—in 1864—established small suburban branches in every direction, with equally satisfactory returns for its enterprise; while the London and County, larger and, perhaps, more cautious than either, also recognised the advantages of suburban expansion. A branch bank belonging to one of these three banks is now to be found in almost every London suburb.

The London and Westminster Bank (established in 1834) was the first in the field, but the atmosphere of the City is not favourable to progress, and the Westminster, though an exceptionally strong and well-managed bank, undoubtedly failed to move with the times. So, too, did the London Joint Stock Bank and the Union Bank of London, which has recently somewhat altered its name. It was not until the provincial joint stock banks invaded London that these companies began to realise the opportunity they had missed; Lloyd's and Parr's Banks however, evidently taking in the situation, adopted the new system, and by skilful amalgamations rapidly forced themselves to the front. The country banks, in short, practically took possession of Lombard Street.

Why the Bank of England did not share the same fate as the private bankers has already been demonstrated. It certainly was not one whit better informed than they; and it sympathised with them in their distrust of the intruders, whose speedy downfall it quite expected to witness. That the joint stock banks must come to grief was the opinion of the majority of City men in 1834, and the then directors of the Bank were City men imbued with those tenets which found credence within the sacred square mile.

The bank which keeps the Government account must always be a great power in the land. Had that account been removed in 1844, together with the last vestige of monopoly, the Bank—the directors of which shared to the full in that tenacity and narrow-mindedness characteristic of wealthy City merchants, whose businesses, and therefore whose ideas, flow in the narrowest of grooves—must have ceased to be a progressive institution. But no Government has ever hinted at deserting the Bank, whose record, though bristling with mistakes, is one of unbroken integrity; and the public has always looked upon its management as above suspicion. Especially was this the case during the first few decades of the new movement.

The Bank of England had public opinion behind it; and the joint stock banks, concerning whose stability opinion was divided, were not then strong enough to keep their own reserves and to defy the Bank; but when their system had stood the test of time, the Bank opened its doors to them, and the companies meekly bowed to the inevitable—for they were not the power in Lombard Street in those days that they are now.

In the first instance, we found the private bankers grouped around the Bank; and now we see our huge joint stock banking companies in a similar relation to her. They kept their reserves with her when their system was in its infancy, when the Bank of England, as a result of monopoly, was the greatest credit institution in the country. As the companies spread their tentacles throughout the land, accumulating credit at an extremely rapid pace, those reserves grew proportionately, until, to-day, we find the Bank of England in the centre of a system which owes over £910,000,000 in *cash* to the public.

Our modern credit system has developed around the Bank, which, as the holder of the bankers' reserves, now occupies an almost national position. That position is, undoubtedly, the indirect result of a monopoly which, prior to 1826, enabled the Bank of England to build up a huge business unopposed by others of its kind. In other words, it had a start of 132 years. The greater, consequently, attracted the smaller. But united Lombard Street is now a much greater power than Threadneedle Street—therefore it is always wise to remember that the Bank of England can only retain its position in the centre of the money market so long as Lombard Street is agreed that it shall.

The banks are not legally obliged to keep their reserves with the Bank of England. Were they so inclined, they could withdraw them to-morrow and accumulate stores of the precious metals of their own. It follows, therefore, that the best of feeling should exist between the "Old Lady" and Lombard Street. Obviously she is not now in a position to dictate her own terms, as her greatest power is derived from the "bankers' balances" on the left-hand side of her balance sheet.

Perhaps it is now easier to understand that the Bank of England, when it from time to time states the lowest rate at which it will discount bills for outsiders, occupies the position of a most important lender, whose minimum rate, though not always the market rate, is seldom either greatly above or below those of its rivals.

CHAPTER XI.
THE LONDON MONEY MARKET.

IT is usual, when describing the Money Market, to assert that it consists of the numerous banks in the City of London; but it seems to me that, in reality, the money market extends throughout the United Kingdom, for wherever there is a bank or a branch bank there is a market for money. Moreover, the demand arising for loanable capital in the provinces largely influences the rates of interest ruling from time to time in London, because, if demand is brisk in the country, the banks have less to lend in London, consequently the rate advances there.

When reference is made to the money market the London short loan fund is invariably meant, and we now have to consider how this fund is formed. The banks, which are liable to the public for huge sums of money at call and short notice, are obliged to keep a certain proportion of cash in their tills and strong rooms and with the Bank of England in order to be prepared for any sudden demand that may be made upon them.

Their cash in hand is, of course, required to meet the ordinary demands of a banking business, and that deposited with the Bank of England is held as a reserve fund against those risks of withdrawal from which a credit institution owing immense sums at call is never free. Roughly speaking, a well-managed bank would keep, say, six per cent. of its public liabilities in legal tender on the premises, and a further ten to twelve per cent. at its credit in the books of the Bank of England. The latter accumulation might be called the bank's *real* reserve, for it is upon this that it would have to rely during a run.

Secondly, from eighteen to thirty per cent. of its liabilities to the public would be invested in first class securities. Those of and guaranteed by the British Government are in great request for this purpose, as the Bank of England would not hesitate to advance against such investments should a company find itself compelled to meet a sudden drain upon its resources. Every prudent banker therefore takes care that a large proportion of these securities is included in his list, which would also contain Metropolitan and other Corporation Stocks, English Railway Debentures, Colonial Government Securities, and so on. A banker's list, in short, should be a so-called "gilt-edged" one.

Thirdly, a banker lends a certain proportion of his deposits in the London money market. Some banks have eight per cent. there, some fourteen per cent., and others from fifteen to twenty per cent., though the larger and better managed companies generally employ from seven to fourteen per cent. therein. A certain amount of this "call money," however, represents money which has been lent to jobbers and brokers on the Stock Exchange for "carrying over" purposes at the various settlements, but by far the larger part of it is money which has been lent to the bill brokers and discount houses.

In no sense can this asset in the balance sheets of the banks be looked upon as a reserve. It is money invested in the London short loan market—money lent to the bill brokers, who, in times of bad credit, might not be able to repay it on demand. Just at the very moment when bankers are most in need, this asset is the least available; therefore, it is about the worst possible form in which the reserve of a credit institution, owing large sums at call, can be invested.

As a credit bank's debts are due at call and short notice, a true reserve can only consist of legal tender, and the till money, which is required in the ordinary course of business during normal times, certainly cannot be classed with that reserve. When considering what is a bank's real cash reserve, we ought to deduct from four to five per cent. from the ratio of cash in hand and with the Bank of England to liabilities, for a trader would not include the cash required from day to day in his business with any reserve he might accumulate against accidents.

Reverting to investments, we might take Consols as an illustration of their liquidity. During normal times Consols can be sold for cash at any moment, but it is otherwise in a time of panic, when practically everybody wants either to sell them or to borrow upon them. The market is then disorganised, and people require either gold or large credits at their bankers—not securities. Hence, even Consols are unsaleable when a panic develops into a crisis.

As the Bank of England holds the cash reserve of the nation, it alone can advance against securities in the midst of a crisis, and those banks which were caught short would then have to apply to the Bank for help. The Bank certainly would not lend upon any but gilt-edged securities during a time of stress, and if their customers then made a call upon them those companies which held second-rate investments would have to close their doors, as they could not obtain assistance from any other source. A strong list of securities is, therefore, essential to every bank that is anxious to protect its customers against disaster.

These three assets (cash in hand and at the Bank of England, money at call and notice, and investments) constitute a bank's so-called liquid assets. The ratio of total liquid assets to liabilities maintained by the best English banks ranges from 43 to 78 per cent. The last-named figures, which are quite exceptional in their strength, were published by Stuckey's Banking Company. The remainder of a bank's resources is employed in making advances and loans, and in discounting bills for its clients, whilst a small proportion is locked up in premises.

We can now form some idea as to what the short loan fund of the London money market really is. Immense sums are collected at the head offices of the banks in London through their metropolitan and provincial branches; and, as the demands of trade are always uncertain—now brisk, then slack—it is impossible for them to invest all their surplus capital in securities; consequently, a certain portion of it finds remunerative employment in this channel.

A huge stream of credit is constantly circulating through the three kingdoms, and London, so to speak, is the heart of the system. In years of active or good trade this stream increases in volume, and during years of depression it contracts; yet it is difficult to say whether or not the resources of the banks (the floating capital of the country) are appreciably lessened during a period of temporary depression, although the national turnover unquestionably is, as may be seen by the Clearing House returns. During years of rising prices and increasing trade activity profits are augmented, and, consequently, the resources of the banks are swollen; but when the profits are invested within the country, a similar amount of credit is returned to the banks by those who have sold their securities, and though less capital is created when trade is dull, it is questionable whether the resources of the banks then shrink very greatly, unless foreign securities are largely purchased.

We have seen that this stream of credit flows to London, and as demand throughout the country is not sufficiently strong to attract it all back again, a large fund of loanable capital accumulates in the hands of the London banks, and flows from them to the bill brokers, who employ it in discounting bills of exchange. But though by far the greater part of the London short loan fund is accumulated in this manner by the banks, other firms and companies also discharge their surplus capital into it. The pool, of course, is not a stagnant one, for capital is constantly flowing in and out.

The India Council, for instance, lends large sums in the London short loan market. The numerous foreign and colonial banks in London do the same, and so, too, do many of the large insurance companies and merchants, while during slack times money finds its way from the Stock Exchange to the bill broking houses. At first sight it seems strange that bankers should advance money to the bill brokers, and so provide their rivals with capital with which to compete against them, especially as the banks have discount departments of their own.

Let us, however, consider the position of the bill broker in relation to the Bank of England and the money market.

Towards the beginning of the nineteenth century the broker acted as agent for the country bankers, but this connection was naturally severed when the country firms opened accounts with the London bankers, and the broker, whose knowledge of bills was extensive, then transacted business for himself. Through holding out for high rates, the London private bankers drove a large amount of business into the hands of the bill brokers, who, by confining their attention solely to this class of credit document, came to be largely trusted by the joint stock companies, which could not obtain servants with the special training of their rivals.

In no other country has the bill broker such influence as in England. In Paris, for instance, the customer discounts with his banker, who re-discounts with the Bank of France; but in London, for reasons already stated, bills find their way to the bill brokers, who re-discount either with the banks or with the Bank of England. Moreover, all the best bills get into the hands of the bill brokers, who, at one time, only discounted the acceptances of the banks and the larger houses; but they now take small trade bills, and, should the banking business grow less profitable, it is questionable whether the banks might not endeavour to dispense with the middleman whom they now encourage.

We next have to consider the London money market as a whole. First we find a system which comprises Lombard Street and Threadneedle Street. In other words, the London banks, by keeping accounts with the Bank of England (Threadneedle Street), have placed that institution in the centre of the system, and we know the Bank derives great power from this situation; but its power is not innate—it is derived through and is dependent upon Lombard Street. This group we will call "the money market" or "the market."

Then we have the bill brokers, of whom we will speak as "the outside market." Every morning the bill broker goes from bank to bank inquiring at what rates he can borrow; and if Lombard Street (the London banks) cannot supply him with all the capital he requires, then he is compelled to apply to the Bank of England, which, however, he always endeavours to avoid, because the Bank invariably charges him a higher rate than do the other banks.

The Bank of England is a great bank of discount: consequently, the brokers are its rivals; so it is hardly reasonable to expect the Bank to charge the same rates to them as to its own clients, seeing that the brokers, by their competition, reduce the Bank's business. When trade is brisk loanable capital is in considerable demand, and the banks, therefore, have less money to lend to the bill brokers, who consequently are then driven to the Bank, which holds the bankers' balances.

But the Bank of England's position is an extremely delicate one; and when the resources of Lombard Street are temporarily exhausted and demand centres upon itself, it has to take care that its ratio of reserve of notes and cash in the Banking Department does not sink too low in proportion to its liabilities. Should the demand upon its resources prove considerable, it raises its rate until the pressure is reduced. As a large part of the trade of this country is conducted through the medium of bills of exchange, it is absolutely essential that there should always be a market for good bills. Otherwise, panic and failures would be the result; so, were the Bank to refuse to take bills from the brokers at a price, our credit system would collapse at once, unless the banks themselves, determined to crush the brokers, offered to deal direct with the holders. But the experiment would be a most risky one to make. Moreover, it could not be attempted at a critical moment. When Lombard Street is not lending freely, or cannot lend further with comparative safety, the Bank, by raising its rate of discount from time to time, reduces the merchant's profit on each transaction, until at last money becomes so dear that he finds that he is making little or no profit on his goods. He therefore produces less, and, consequently, discounts less, when the pressure upon the Bank relaxes.

So long as money may be obtained, let the price paid for it be what it may, a sense of security pervades the community; but were it whispered during a period of temporary tightness that the Bank refused to discount good bills at any price, our credit system would be in imminent danger, for the trade of the country would be at a standstill. Further, did such a state of affairs continue for many days, the crash would come, and the Bank of England would then be swept away with the rest of the market. Our present system is so delicately poised that the Bank simply dare not refuse to take good trade bills from the brokers.

We next come to the other side of the picture. The broker, when he goes his rounds, sometimes finds that the surplus resources of the banks are abundant, and that they are ready to let him have even more than he requires. When he makes this discovery, he begins to higgle, to try to ascertain the lowest rate certain banks are prepared to accept; for the difference between the rate at which he discounts bills for his own customers and the rate at which he re-discounts or borrows, is his margin of profit, and he is naturally anxious to make it as wide as possible. (The poor man, be it remembered, does not visit Lombard Street simply because he finds the air pure and the society of bank officials congenial.) He therefore does his best to discover those banks which are in funds, and, having found them, to induce them to lend as cheaply as possible. This he can do when loanable capital is cheap and abundant, and the Bank of England probably doing but little business. Possibly, though the Bank rate is at two and a half, bills are being taken by the brokers at one and a half. Then the Bank, in order to get business, either lowers its rate of discount or else, by selling stock, endeavours to lessen the resources of Lombard Street.

If the Bank adopt the latter expedient, it usually sells Consols for cash, and buys them back for the account, thereby temporarily reducing "bankers' balances," and attracting business to itself. The banks, having less to lend, raise their rates, which then approximate more closely to the Bank rate.

The brokers often complain bitterly of this interference by the Bank of England with the market's supply of loanable capital, asserting that this artificial enhancement of rates by the reduction of bankers' balances through the sale of stock affects their business injuriously, and benefits the Bank but little; and it certainly is difficult to see how the Bank of England can make a profit out of the transaction.

On the other hand, when the market rate is appreciably below the Bank rate, it is impossible to attract foreign gold to London; and the Bank, by borrowing on Consols, and making its rate representative, is acting in the public interest, should it be desirable either to attract gold to this country or to prevent its leaving these shores. We can now see that the Bank of England, though it states its minimum rate, is often powerless to transact business thereat; and, recognising that its own rate is out of touch with the market rate, the Bank often discounts bills for its own customers at the rates ruling in the open market, as, were it to refuse to do so, its clients would naturally take their bills to the cheapest house. When, however, Lombard Street is empty, and the bill brokers are compelled to approach the Bank which holds the final reserve, the Bank of England is frequently in a position to charge its rivals one per cent. above its declared minimum, and the bill brokers quite naturally feel a little sore. For this reason they try every source of supply before making application to the Bank. As security against loans made to them the brokers usually deposit either bills which they have discounted in the ordinary course of their business or gilt-edged securities, but sometimes the bill broker's credit is so good that the banks lend him money at call practically without security. When securities are deposited they are of course returned directly the loan is paid off.

There is also another little point to which attention may be drawn: to wit—that, although the market we are discussing is a special market, yet if a borrower's credit be good it is generally possible to obtain an advance either at or about Bank rate.

CHAPTER XII.
THE BANK RATE AND STOCK EXCHANGE SECURITIES.

AT the present time large advances are made by the banking companies to members of the Stock Exchange, and it is supposed that at the beginning of 1894, when the Bank rate fell to two per cent., and an investment of surplus funds in the London short loan market brought in very poor returns, the banks, tempted by higher rates, largely increased their loans to the Stock Exchange. In 1890 rumour had it that a few of the banks made rather heavy losses in connection with the South American gamble, which brought down the firm of Barings; and the unanimity they displayed, under the leadership of the late Mr. Lidderdale, in supporting the tottering structure, certainly lends force to the suggestion; for philanthropists are not to be found either in Lombard Street or in Gorgonzola Hall.

The same rumour was circulated after the Kaffir boom in 1895, and a little later it was whispered that some of the banks intended curtailing their loans to the Stock Exchange, and that in future mining shares would be received with the greatest circumspection. So close is the connection between the banks and the "House" that the utmost consternation prevailed when it was feared that the banks would not touch certain stocks and shares of a fluctuating character. The mere rumour created almost a panic among those dealers whose books were full of the tabooed securities.

But 1895 was a bad year for the banking companies, and, from a dividend point of view, 1896 was little better, for the Bank rate did not touch two-and-a-half per cent. until September of that year. The short loan market, therefore, was not a tempting place into which to pour surplus deposits, so the banks apparently thought better of their decision (if it were a decision), and continued their loans to the Stock Exchange on the same liberal scale, because such loans yielded a much better return than those to the bill brokers.

The very rumour that the banks intended increasing their margin on, say, American Rails, would cause those securities to fall, and were the threat actually executed, then, unless strong support came either from the public or from New York, the result would be failures of weak jobbers in that particular market, and a heavy fall in the prices of American Railway securities. There is the same link between the other markets of the Stock Exchange and the banks, and, such being the case, it naturally follows that the prices of securities are influenced by the abundance or scarcity of loanable capital, and that, therefore, continuation rates fluctuate with the Bank rate.

But a very considerable proportion of the transactions conducted on the Stock Exchange is of a speculative or gambling nature, in which those mysterious persons called "bulls" and "bears" figure largely, and whose object it is, not to invest savings in particular stocks and shares, but to receive a cheque from their broker representing differences due to them on the rise or fall of the securities in which they are temporarily interested.

The "bull" buys stock because he believes that it will rise, and that he will be able to sell it at a profit before the fortnightly settlement comes round, but he does not pay for it; and if his sanguine anticipation is not realised, so human and hopeful is he, that he endeavours to obtain a loan on his stock through his broker in order to carry it over to the next settlement, trusting that he will be able to sell at a profit before contango day again comes round. The broker sometimes obtains an advance on the stock through his banker, and so is enabled to accommodate his client, whom he charges both interest and commission. Again, the broker may carry over the stock through a jobber or with a money broker who is a member of the "House," as the Stock Exchange is colloquially called.

It has been suggested that some of these money brokers are in reality agents of the banks—that, in short, they are the middlemen between the banks and those who want to borrow on the Stock Exchange, just as the bill broker is the middleman between the banks and those persons who possess bills. The bill broker deposits the bills he has discounted for his customers as security against a loan from the banker, and the money broker deposits the stocks and shares against which he has advanced to members of the Stock Exchange as security for a loan from the banker to himself. His profit, therefore, like that of the bill broker, would be the difference between the rate at which he borrows from the banker and the rate at which he lends in the House. When large sums are advanced in this manner the prices of stocks and shares are forced up to fictitious figures in the hope that the public will come in and buy. Yet the Stock Exchange Committee preaches about the iniquities of the outside broker! Far be it from me to defend the possibly questionable methods of the latter; but, to an unbiased observer, it sounds somewhat like the pot calling the kettle black.

Huge sums of money are advanced every fortnight by the banks to the money brokers and jobbers, principally against sold stocks and shares, which are awaiting the arrival of *bonâ fide* investors. The banks, of course, require a good margin in order to cover themselves against loss through any possible depreciation in the hypothecated securities, and when the settlement or day of reckoning arrives, fresh loans are made, or old advances are renewed, and the securities carried over to the end of the account. A high rate of interest naturally makes "carrying over" from account to account a very expensive operation, whilst an abnormally high rate renders the process prohibitive.

When, therefore, the Bank rate is high and money is dear, a check is immediately given to speculation on the Stock Exchange, because those persons who have bought securities for a rise prefer to sell at a loss before the settlement rather than pay excessive contango rates. It follows, then, that dear money greatly reduces the dimensions of the accounts open for the rise.

The banks, too, often become alarmed by the magnitude of the account, and having demands upon them for capital elsewhere, they grow nervous and lend less freely, at greatly enhanced rates, and then jobbers and money brokers have to refuse a large number of applicants. The result may be either a fall in the securities dealt in by a particular market or a general depression throughout the House. Then the "bears" come in and buy, take their profits, and are jubilant.

Conversely, a plethora of money and a low Bank rate encourage speculation, as was the case before the boom of 1895. Continuation rates are low, and capital comes out of trade into the better-class securities, which begin to rise in consequence. Then, for a little while, the "bulls" have it all their own way. But why does the Committee pose as the friend of the *bonâ fide* investor? It is a little difficult to see where he comes in, unless it be in at the top and out at the bottom. As a matter of fact, there is so much gambling in securities taking place in the House that the genuine investor, if he do not understand the market, falls an easy prey to the "bulls" and "bears," who, by studying the habits of his kind, anticipate their requirements, and, after taking a large bite, pass on their hypothecated shares. On the other hand, the investor who studies the markets sometimes waits patiently for exhausted "bulls" or sells to frightened "bears." So, to those who know the game it is about as broad as it is long.

CHAPTER XIII.
THE BANKS AS STOCKBROKERS.

WERE business on the Stock Exchange solely of an investment nature, it has been suggested that that institution could dispense with over fifty per cent. of its members, for, during recent years, a large amount of the investment business of the country has drifted to the banks, which place their orders in the hands of a few brokers, with whom they divide the usual one-eighth per cent. commission. The large banking companies are outside brokers, and so eager are some of them to attract this class of business that they offer their clerks half the commission received from the broker upon all business introduced by them. Seeing that the average bank clerk is absolutely without experience of the markets, touts of this variety are a source of danger to the public.

The banker who divides his share of the commission with the clerk who introduces the business is satisfied with one-thirty-second per cent. commission; but the broker, who only gets one-sixteenth instead of one-eighth per cent., is, probably, less eager to make a close bargain for a customer of the bank than for one of his own. On the other hand, the volume of investment business which flows through the banks to the Stock Exchange is so large that those brokers who are favoured with the banks' custom must earn considerable sums by way of commission. Whether orders from customers of the banks receive that individual attention which the brokers give to those from their own clients is, however, another matter.

Most of the banks have Stock Departments, to which orders are sent by their country branches. These orders are steadily increasing, and the tendency seems to be for a large number of the provincial public to do their investment business through the banks. This class of business is, therefore, gradually drifting to the banks, and doubtless, as time goes on, the banking companies will become the recognised channel for the *bonâ fide* country investor.

It follows that the non-speculative business is getting into a few hands, with the result that a large number of brokers on the Stock Exchange are, so to speak, "starved," and consequently obliged to turn their attention to the demand created by the more speculatively disposed members of the public. Yet, strange to say, in spite of the fact that orders are now diverted to the Stock Departments of the London banks and that, therefore, fewer brokers are required to transact the investment business of the country, the members of the Stock Exchange are increasing numerically. Seeing that the safe business is drifting through the banks into the hands of a few large brokers we may well ask how the smaller men obtain a living from their business?

The ground, year in year out, is being farmed assiduously by the banks, whose large capital and established credit inspire widespread confidence; and in the face of such competition the small broker's chance of success does not seem encouraging. How can he make a business? The banks, who place their orders with strong brokers, guarantee those customers who deal through them against the insolvency of both the broker and the jobber, and such a guarantee is unquestionably worth having. The small broker, as a rule, possesses very little capital; whereas the person who instructs his banker either to buy or to sell is conscious that he is dealing through an institution whose credit is practically unlimited, and whose resources amount to many millions. He has not, therefore, to ask himself whether his broker is safe, and this sense of security, inspired by a bank's millions, undoubtedly causes many people who would rather do business direct with a member of the Stock Exchange to deal with the banks. Moreover, a bank official is quite well aware of this advantage, and when a customer, who is undecided whether or not to employ a broker, asks what inducement the bank holds out to him, he quietly replies: "You have the bank's credit upon which to rely." Such an answer makes a customer reflect. Further, it seldom fails to effect its purpose, because, in the first place, it instils a doubt in the client's mind regarding the means of his broker; and, in the second place, because he cannot fail to recognise the greater security the bank affords him.

It is evident, then, that the small broker's path is bestrewn with almost insuperable difficulties, and that it is extremely hard for him to attract safe business. But the banking companies do not arrest the flow of speculative orders to his books.

The banks, which have a horror of speculation, confine their attention to the buying and selling of stocks and shares through their brokers. Were they to encourage gambling in securities they are fully aware that the result would be disastrous to the business of banking, for a certain number of their customers would be sure to neglect their business in the hope of snatching differences on the Stock Exchange, and such a policy would end in a crisis that would bring the country to the verge of ruin. For this reason alone the banks firmly and wisely refuse to foster speculation among their clients.

Capital, we all know, is the savings of labour; consequently the greater the profits made in trade during any one year, the larger is the fund awaiting investment. Now, if the banks were to incite the gambling fever among their customers, this fund would tend to diminish each year, and, seeing that the prosperity of the country is entirely dependent upon its trade, bankers, customers, and stockbrokers would speedily become involved in common ruin. Small wonder, then, that our large banking companies, which are responsible to the public for millions of money—a large proportion of which they must be prepared to return at any moment—decline to open speculative accounts for their clients. It would be madness on the part of such institutions to divert their customers' attention from trade to speculation in securities; and for this reason the bank clerk as amateur commission agent seems a step in the wrong direction.

Moreover, in this respect the policy of the banks appears contradictory. Recognising the temptations to which their clerks are exposed, it is their practice to instantly dismiss those men who indulge a passion for betting; yet some of them deliberately encourage their servants to tout for investment orders, apparently unconscious of the fact that once their attention is drawn to the markets, some of the clerks are almost certain to end by gambling for differences on their own account. Helping themselves to the money of the banks is probably the next step. Were not the question so serious, the fact that directors cannot make so palpable a deduction would be positively humorous, for it is evidently quite as undesirable, from their point of view, that a clerk should bet upon a stock as upon a horse.

The modern credit system, it will be seen, places a very large part of the safe or investment business in the hands of a minority of brokers, who, like the bankers, much prefer to do a good commission business, and to leave speculation to the smaller brokers, who have less to lose than they. These favoured brokers have grown accustomed to sleeping comfortably o' nights, undisturbed by the vision of settling day on the morrow; and, quite blind to the cause of their enviable freedom from care, they are disposed to be loud in their abuse of the risky manner in which some of the smaller brokers conduct their business. But, seeing that the non-speculative orders flow from the banks to themselves, it would be interesting if they would attempt to explain how the army of small brokers can live unless they cater for the wants of the speculator. As a rule their capital is small, consequently they cannot afford to wait years while they slowly build up a connection; so, as the safe business is cornered, they accept the risky. This they do, not from choice, but from necessity; and the Stock Exchange Committee, in order to prevent additions to the ranks of these undesirables, should take steps to reduce the number of members of the Stock Exchange very considerably. Already the investors of this country have to support a small army of over four thousand of them.

Of course, after every period of excitement, numerous weak members of the Stock Exchange are weeded out, and, in a sense, the *bonâ fide* investor is the pigeon that is plucked by the speculator. The bulls buy in the fond hope that the investor will come in and relieve them of their stock; and the bears sell securities which they do not possess, trusting that investors will also sell, thereby enabling them to buy at a low figure and to pass on their securities at a profit to those to whom they have previously sold. The position is therefore often an artificial one, created by operators for the rise or fall, and the investor, unless he thoroughly understands the markets, is like a pigeon among hawks.

The larger the number of members of the House, the greater is the risk run by the investor who deals with a small broker; and as the investment business of the country flows largely in a particular channel, it is more than probable that, unless the Committee decides to admit new members sparingly, a large number of small brokers will one day be "hammered" after a period of intense excitement.

CHAPTER XIV.
THE SHORT LOAN FUND AND THE PRICE OF SECURITIES.

A CERTAIN proportion of the capital which flows into the London short loan fund is invested in securities by the bill brokers and the discount houses, and, as the said securities are deposited with the bankers from time to time against temporary advances, it follows that their choice is largely restricted to those of and guaranteed by the British Government, because the margin exacted on the so-called gilt-edged varieties is considerably less than that demanded upon the more fluctuating stocks and shares.

The bankers themselves invest largely in the same class, and they also employ vast sums in the short loan market; so that when the market rate for bills is higher than the interest received upon, say, Consols, the bankers are disposed to sell some of their Consols in order to obtain the higher rates ruling in the outside market. Obviously, then, any accretion or diminution in the short loan fund at once affects the prices of gilt-edged securities. If the Bank rate be high, and also representative, Consols ought to fall, and, conversely, if the Bank of England's rate be low, trade dull, and the market rate of discount smaller than the return on Consols, gilt-edged securities should rise.

If this be the case, a low Bank rate must give an immediate incentive to speculation in securities, and, therefore, the condition of the short loan fund is intimately connected with the prices of stocks and shares, but more particularly with those securities in which lenders in the money market largely invest. The banks—let the condition of the money market be what it may—must, of course, always invest a certain proportion of their resources in Consols, but the sum so invested is not constant.

Again, powerful business firms and companies hold Government stock as reserves against contingencies. The Government makes large purchases in the Consol market on account of the Post Office Savings Bank and the Sinking Fund, while numerous other "bull" points could be given. However, the fact remains that cheap money provides a strong inducement to large speculative purchases of Consols.

The large capitalists and those persons whose credit is good can borrow at, and sometimes even slightly below, Bank rate on Consols from the banks, which are satisfied with a small margin against possible depreciation on Government securities. If, therefore, we examine the period between

February, 1894, and September, 1896, when the Bank rate was stationary at two per cent., it will be possible to illustrate this tendency. Day-to-day money was then sometimes quoted at one per cent. and under, and this state of affairs occasionally extended over protracted periods.

Now, suppose a person invested £20,000 in Consols at 112, and that his banker agreed to advance £18,000 against them at, say, seven days' notice at one per cent. per annum. Two-and-three-quarter Consols at 112 return £2 9s. per cent. (about). His annual income, therefore, on £20,000 would amount to about £490; but he owed his banker one per cent. on £18,000. Hence £180 must be deducted from £490. Upon a capital of £2000 he therefore earned £310; and a return of fifteen-and-a-half per cent. per annum on Consols is surely an excellent reward for his skill. Of course, we must not forget possible depreciation; but seeing that the banker's advance released £18,000, which he can use, he can afford to take some risk.

The following example, however, affords a more practical illustration of the possibilities of speculation in Consols during the depressed portion of a cycle, when the prices of commodities are low and loanable capital is cheap. First, we want to ascertain the movements in this security from, say, 1894 to 1896, and of these the table given hereunder supplies a good idea:—

	1894.	1895.	1896.	
Goschen's Two-and-three-quarters per cent. (Two-and-a-half per cent. 5th April, 1903)	Highest. 103⅝	Highest. 108⅛	Highest. 114	Bank rate from 22nd Feb., 1894, to 9th Sept., 1896.
	Lowest. 98⅜	Lowest. 103½	Lowest. 105⅛	Two per cent.

Let us assume that a person invested £20,000 in Consols at parity in 1894, and arranged with his banker for a loan against them at Bank rate, and that the banker's margin was to be ten per cent. on the purchase price. He received, then, a loan of £18,000 from his banker, so the amount of his own capital remaining in the venture was £2000. Very probably, especially if his credit were beyond doubt, he would have made a closer bargain with his banker, and thus have reduced the margin slightly—but this is by the way.

Upon his £20,000 in Consols he obtained two-and-three-quarters per cent., so that his annual income therefrom was £550. But as he had to pay his banker two per cent. per annum on £18,000, £360 must be deducted from £550. His capital in the speculation being £2000, he made £190 thereupon. This gain works out at nine-and-a-half per cent. per annum, and nine-and-a-half per cent. on Consols may surely be classed among the minor forms of temptation. Moreover, as the Bank rate stood at two per cent. for slightly over two years and a half, he had a long run for his money.

But we see that he bought at parity, and that in 1896 Consols touched 114. Had he sold at 110 during that year, his £20,000 in Consols would have realised £22,000. He, however, owed his banker £18,000, so there remained £4000 to his credit. As his own capital in the speculation was £2000 he would have exactly doubled it, and nine-and-a-half per cent. per annum upon £2000 in Consols for close upon two years, with a bonus of £2000 at the finish, is painfully reminiscent of those financial dreams which so very seldom materialise; yet huge blocks of Consols were actually bought during this period of two per cent., and dealt with in the manner aforesaid.

Of course, the results were not always so satisfactory as those given in the above illustrations, and no doubt many such ventures ended in a loss, for prizes of this description are for the lucky few; though it is usual to dwell upon them to the mortification of the mutable many. The snatching of profits in this fashion requires skill and considerable patience, and those persons who receive specious pamphlets telling them how money is to be made in a marvellously short space of time by an infallible system may appreciate the plausibility of my illustrations, but yet should remember that they may find the results of similar speculations in Consols very disappointing.

The demand for Government securities created by these speculative operations is one of the causes which drive up the price of Consols during periods of cheap money, but it is not by any means the only cause. When the Bank rate advances, and capital can be employed more advantageously in the London short loan market, this period soon comes to an end, and consequent sales depress the Consol market.

Very many of the better class securities such as Colonial Government stocks, Foreign Government securities, and so on, yield from three to five per cent., and when the Bank of England rate is at from two to two and a half, though the margin demanded upon such stocks is wider than that required upon Consols, the difference between the interest received in the shape of dividends and that paid as the price of a loan often makes speculative dealings in them decidedly profitable. As the Bank rate increases, and the speculator's profit margin consequently narrows, the tendency is for stocks and shares so "carried" to fall in value. The holders or gamblers then begin to sell, and as the increased supply of such securities is certain not to be met by an enhanced demand on the part of investors, prices must fall. Seeing the better class securities declining in value, those investors who had previously held aloof are tempted to come in, and the greater the reaction, the stronger is the inducement to buy; consequently, the lower prices recede the larger becomes the number of purchasers, until demand overtakes supply and prices again begin to move upwards.

Broadly speaking, it is evident that, unless the markets are disorganised by panic or by some disquieting political occurrence, the prices of the so-called gilt-edged securities are influenced by the conditions prevailing in the London short loan money market.

CHAPTER XV.
PANIC YEARS.

WHEN in 1667 a Dutch fleet sailed up the Medway, demolished a fort at Sheerness, and, forcing a way into Chatham Docks, burnt all the ships assembled therein, to the consternation of the inhabitants of London, there was a run upon the banks; but a Stuart regarded both events with equanimity, for "Old Rowley" had a mind above trifles of this description, possibly because he had learnt many bitter truths in a world seldom understood by Kings. Cynics are not born—they are made; and Charles II. had drunk from that cup which sharpens the understanding.

France, during 1719 and 1720, was in the throes of the Mississippi scheme, which was engineered by that notorious Scotsman, John Law; and England, in 1720, witnessed the collapse of the South Sea Company, which Sir Robert Walpole, with rare insight and unerring financial instinct, had demonstrated was a mere gamble, that, at the best, could only enjoy a temporary success, which was absolutely dependent upon a rise in the company's stock; but the Government turned a deaf ear to his warning.

Scotland, we have seen, had its Darien venture in 1699; and in 1720 all England went mad over the South Sea Company, which offered to relieve the Government of part of the National Debt, and entered into an insane competition with the Bank of England for that purpose. Then occurred some spirited bidding between the two companies for this privilege; but the directors of the Bank proved themselves the less mad, and left their rival in possession of the incubus and the road to ruin.

The result of the bidding gave the necessary stimulus to the South Sea Company's stock, and, seeing it going up, the public at once rushed in, when the stock rose faster than ever. In a very short space of time the fever for speculation infused itself into the blood of the whole nation. The pace became so furious that the more thoughtful among the gamblers began to see the end and to sell, with the result that, upon a memorable morning, everybody wanted to dispose of his stock—and then the bubble burst.

In June, 1720, the £100 stock of the South Sea Company was rushed up to £890, and a little later it touched £1000. Then the tide turned, and, as is invariably the case, all were as anxious to sell as a few days before they had been eager to buy. Every hour intensified the panic, until at length the stock fell to £175, and the difference between the highest and lowest quotations is eloquent of the loss inflicted upon the community, for everybody who had money to invest was interested in this gigantic gamble.

Widespread misery and ruin followed. Suicide was of daily occurrence, and, after a momentary lull in the storm, popular indignation lashed itself into fury against the directors, for whom, it was openly declared, hanging was too good a fate. The Government, thoroughly alarmed, turned to the one strong man who had consistently opposed the scheme, and who, in consequence, was at that moment the most popular man in England; so Sir Robert Walpole stepped into the breach, and stemmed the tide of popular indignation and national disaster.

At first Walpole was disposed to resort to half-measures, but when it became apparent that the South Sea Company was rotten to the core and that it must go at any price, he devised a scheme by which the East India Company and the Bank of England took over £18,000,000 of South Sea stock. The Bank directors, throughout this trying period, acted with a strange lack of caution, and the situation was only saved by Walpole's better judgment.

The period was one of mad speculation, and no venture was too absurd to foist upon a public, which, until the crash came, did not display a gleam of intelligence or discernment, so blinded was it by greed. Naturally, those bankers who had advanced against South Sea stock did not escape loss, and many of the goldsmiths and private bankers were ruined by the reaction, while the Bank of England itself barely escaped. It is interesting to notice that, even in 1720, the public could only be tempted by a rising market; and it has remained true to this instinct, as, for some unaccountable reason, the "bear" is always looked upon as an undesirable kind of person.

The next disturbance of credit occurred in 1745, when the Young Pretender, "Bonnie Prince Charlie," after defeating Sir John Cope at Prestonpans, resolved to march on London, and penetrated as far as Derby. The news of his arrival there reached London on the 4th December (Black Friday), and the City was seized with so severe a panic that business was suspended. Some of the citizens actually left the country, and even the King made preparations for flight. Everybody then wished to possess himself of gold, and a run at once began upon the Bank of England, which was taken completely by surprise, and only saved the situation by resorting to the expedient of paying its notes in sixpences—a somewhat lengthy proceeding, but one which enabled it to gain time. Nobody, however, would trust a Stuart, and the panic very quickly subsided.

Learning that the Duke of Cumberland was advancing to meet him, Charles was compelled by his followers to beat a hasty retreat towards Scotland, and by the 23rd December the Highlanders had crossed the border again. In January, 1746, they defeated General Hawley at Falkirk, but in the following April the Prince lost the battle of Culloden, which dealt the final blow to the hopes of the House of Stuart.

The panics and crises between 1745 and 1857 have been discussed in Chapters I. and II. of this book—principally in Chapter II.

The Crimean War, through which this country muddled, was brought to a close in 1856, at a cost to the nation of £33,000,000; and it may perhaps be interesting to compare this sum with the £230,000,000 which has been expended in the South African struggle. Even for a Balaclava £33,000,000 seems a dear price to pay. But £230,000,000 for a Colenso! Glory makes a poor national asset.

In 1848 Lord Dalhousie carried out a policy of annexation in India in a ruthless manner, and the native princes, thirsting for revenge, insidiously propagated a rumour among the native soldiery of the East India Company to the effect that the British Government was anxious to Christianise them, knowing that the unsophisticated Hindu preferred his sacred cow to the God of his conquerors, though he had probably little faith in either.

At any rate, the princes appealed to the patriotism of the native soldiers, who, in May, 1857, replied by refusing to accept the famous "greased" cartridges, and in a few days the insurrectionary movement was ablaze in India. The massacre at Cawnpore sent a thrill of horror and indignation through the country, and Sir Colin Campbell (afterwards Lord Clyde) was ordered post haste from England to take command of the British troops. Naturally, our trade with India was disorganised; and, speculation having exceeded all bounds in America, the grave news from that country, combined with the outbreak in India, hastened on the crisis of 1857.

Quite an epidemic of crime swept through England about the middle of the nineteenth century, and many names well known in the City were smirched, whilst even the firm of Overend and Gurney, whose credit was then at its zenith, were said to have compounded a felony in order to avoid a bad debt. Financial morality, which is at all times peculiar, was at this period at its lowest ebb. So small wonder that when the American banks failed by the dozen in 1857, a feeling of distrust should make itself felt in this country, which was then engaged in a fierce struggle in India.

Merchants and houses engaged in trade with India and America began to fail, and in a very little while there was a run upon some of the banks. Then followed the collapse of the Borough Bank, and Dennistoun's of Liverpool. In Scotland the Western Bank and the City of Glasgow Bank put up their shutters; and the failure in London of Sanderson & Co., the well-known bill brokers, accentuated the grave condition of credit, forcibly reminded the public that the rotten state of the American railroads had ruined thousands of speculators in this country, and generated in the public mind a feeling of positive alarm. The result was a panic, which by 12th November culminated in a crisis. The country then looked to the Government and to the Bank of England.

Both 1855 and 1856 were years of unusually high Bank rates, and during 1857 the demand for loanable capital became so pronounced that the Bank of England, in order to protect its dwindling store of bullion, had to raise its rate still further. The year opened with six per cent. In July it fell to five-and-a-half per cent., but by 19th October it had reached eight per cent. On 5th November nine per cent. was recorded; and upon the 9th of the same month it was hurriedly raised to ten per cent. Lombard Street had then practically arrived at the end of its available resources; and demand, of course, centred itself upon the bank which held the bankers' cash balances.

The Bank of England, as usual in those days, was quite unprepared to meet a crisis, and made application for assistance to the Government. Had help then been refused, it must inevitably have closed its doors, for the reserve in its Banking Department on 13th November, 1857, had fallen to £957,000, while it was rumoured that, at the close of a particular day, the reduction was appreciably greater. In plain English, the Bank of England was practically broken.

On 12th November the Government consented, for the second time since 1844, to the suspension of the Bank Charter Act; and when it became known that the Bank of England was in a position to increase its circulation to an unlimited extent, and to advance notes against the better-class securities, the nervous tension created by the numerous failures throughout the country instantly relaxed, and in a few days a comparative calm followed the storm. Indeed, before the close of 1858 the Bank rate was down to two-and-a-half per cent.

The suspension of the Act during a crisis creates a market for securities at the Bank of England. Furthermore, at so critical a moment the Bank is the only market in existence; consequently those securities in which it decides to deal are alone saleable, and we know that it confines its advances solely to the so-called gilt-edged securities and to good bills. Of course, if the public only thought, it would instantly perceive that the more notes the Bank issues in excess of its authorised amount the less secure is its position, because the smaller is the proportion of gold in the Issue Department to its liabilities. But the British public is led; it does not think. If it did we should speedily be in the throes of a revolution.

The public thinks the Government lends its credit to the Bank, but in reality it does nothing of the kind. It simply authorises the Bank of England to break the law, and to advance notes at its discretion. However, the credit of the Bank is so good that the public, seeing that it has the "moral" support of the Government, possesses absolute confidence in its stability; and though it trusts the Bank blindly and unreasonably, that institution has earned its gratitude upon more than one occasion, and its history, if full of mistakes, certainly entitles it to this confidence.

Mention has been made of the failure of the Western Bank of Scotland in 1857. This institution, besides advancing indiscreetly at home, helped to finance the gamble in American securities; consequently, when the crisis occurred in the United States, the bank found itself saddled with huge blocks of unsaleable stocks and shares. Subsequent investigation disclosed a most discreditable state of affairs.

In 1856 the Royal British Bank, after a short life of continual fraud, came to the ground; and in 1857 the public learned that the notorious Colonel Waugh had fled to Spain with considerable sums belonging to the Eastern Banking Company. A little later, when it was discovered that bank directors and auditors who, for a consideration, would attest such statements as those issued by the Western Bank, could be found in Scotland, the public came to the conclusion that a balance sheet is worth little more than the paper upon which it is printed; and a run at once began upon the rest of the Scotch banks, which promptly arrested the panic by guaranteeing the notes of the insolvent Western Bank of Scotland. The City of Glasgow Bank, though it closed its doors temporarily during this period of fraud and distrust, succeeded in weathering the storm, only to fail badly in 1878.

The relations between England and France were severely strained in 1859. A plot was hatched in London by an Italian secret society against the life of Napoleon III., whose publication of a denunciation of British hospitality sent a thrill of passionate resentment through this country, which replied to his threat of invasion by the inception of the volunteer movement. The call met with immediate response, for nothing kindles enthusiasm so quickly as hate, and England, for the first time in her history, created an army of citizen soldiers. At the height of the frenzy there were ominous rumours, and for a little while a state of panic prevailed; but the alarm soon subsided, and the next year a commercial treaty was enacted with France.

During 1862 loanable capital was cheap, and in July that year the Bank rate sank to two per cent., whilst at no time did it exceed three per cent. With money abundant, the promoter was soon in evidence, and the speculation fever once more took possession of the public, hundreds of companies being registered under the Companies Act of 1862 within the space of a few months, until dear money began to lessen the output of limited liability concerns and the energies of that arch-enemy, the promoter. In 1861 the United States was convulsed by civil war, which caused a cessation of production there on a large scale, and produced a cotton famine in this country. Lancashire, the centre of the industry, could not obtain fresh supplies of the raw material when the ports of the Southern States were blockaded, and early in January, 1863, hundreds of thousands of operatives were out of employment. Speculation instantly received a check, and the energies of the country were concentrated upon raising huge sums for the alleviation of the distress in Lancashire—for 500,000 unemployed workers might at any moment, should their attitude become menacing, prove a danger to the State.

From 1863 to 1865 the Bank of England was undoubtedly face to face with a serious situation, and, for the first time in its history, its directors grasped the simple fact that only by maintaining a good reserve can the country be saved from panics and crises. The year 1863 was one of high Bank rates, and during the autumn of 1864 pressure upon the Bank's resources became so severe that a crisis was narrowly averted. Supplies of cotton from America having practically ceased, demand centred upon India, and the Bank of England, early in August, had to support a drain of silver thither to help pay for the cotton crop. On 4th August the Bank rate was raised to eight per cent., and again on 8th September to nine per cent., at which figure it remained until the 10th November, when it fell to eight again. The strain upon the Bank was severe, but the crises of 1847 and 1857 had taught their lesson, and by using the "Bank rate" with effect, the directors succeeded in keeping a sufficient reserve in the Banking Department.

By about the middle of 1865 capital was cheap, but, towards the end of that year, a decided stringency manifested itself, and at the beginning of 1866 many companies which had been registered under the Act of 1862 failed. The banks, whose reserves were then much smaller than now, came in for their share of distrust, and the failure of a Liverpool firm for a large amount made the public uneasy; but when it was known on the 11th May that Overend, Gurney & Co. had closed their doors, the City was seized with panic, and streams of depositors rushed to Lombard Street to withdraw their money from the banks, which, in a very short time, were paying out at a rate it was impossible to maintain; and it soon became evident that unless confidence were speedily restored the banks must break.

The Bank of England had to meet large demands from the provincial banks, for distrust was general throughout the country; consequently at such a moment the country bankers required their reserves of cash in their safes, so that they could immediately meet the demands of the more nervous of their customers should necessity arise. The Bank advanced its rate to seven per cent. on the 3rd May; to eight per cent. on the 8th of the same month; and to nine per cent. on the 11th; and, the pressure becoming more intense, application was made to the Chancellor of the Exchequer, with the result that the Bank of England was authorised to break the Act if necessary, the Government's condition being that the rate of discount should be ten per cent. while the Act was in abeyance; so, on the 12th May, the Bank rate was raised to ten per cent., where it remained until the 16th August following.

By the 16th May the reserve was reduced to £731,000, but directly it became known that the Bank was in a position to advance notes against approved securities the tension relaxed, thereby proving that the public understood the cure as little as it did the disease—for it was an act of madness to make the run, and equally as stupid not to perceive that the issuing of unconvertible notes is at the best only a quack remedy. However, the remedy proved effective, and the result enables one to realise that a nation, like an individual, is the slave of habit.

The history of the firm of Overend, Gurney & Co. makes sorry reading. Between this old-established discount house and the Bank of England there had always existed a spirit of rivalry; and when, after the crisis of 1857, the Bank stated its intention not to again assist the bill brokers during a time of panic, and only to make advances to them at those periods when the Government takes large sums off the market, a very bitter feeling sprang up between the discount houses and the Bank.

Overends, determined to show the Bank that it was not omnipotent, allowed their account at the Bank of England to run largely into credit, and one day suddenly demanded three millions in cash. Their ruse failed. Indeed it was as stupid as the resolution which goaded them into making the effort; for, of course, were the Bank to refuse to assist the bill brokers during a panic, it would only be adding fuel to the flames and increasing its own difficulties. Small wonder then that so absurd a decree created intense irritation, for, upon examination, it is evident that the Bank of England is as dependent upon the bankers' balances in a time of panic as are the bill brokers upon the institution which holds them. Then what folly to advertise such a decision!

Naturally, the Bank is not pleased at the thought that it must help its rivals over the stile, but the peculiarities of our banking system compel it to, whether it like the task or not. Therefore, it was an error of judgment on the part of the directors of the Bank to pose as the champions of the banking community, and to declare that the bill brokers must, in future, accumulate reserves of their own, when they knew quite well that the nature of their business utterly precluded such an attempt.

During a panic the Bank of England can only save itself by advancing freely against certain securities and good bills. The credit so created, however, swells the bankers' balances in its own books, and consequently the amount standing to the credit of the bankers increases appreciably. But, at such a moment, the bankers call in large sums from the bill brokers, and, unless the brokers can obtain advances from the Bank of England against good bills and gilt-edged securities, they will be unable to satisfy the demands of Lombard Street. By declining to advance to the bill brokers, the Bank, in reality, would be refusing credit to Lombard Street (bankers' balances); and, as the Bank itself could not live were Lombard Street to withdraw its balances at so critical a time, it follows that it must lend to the bill brokers in order to enable them to repay the bankers. It simply dare not refuse to assist them, for, if it did, the banks might decline to support the Bank which left them in the lurch just at the height of the storm. The bill brokers (the outside market) come within our present credit system, and if, when a state of panic prevails, they were left to their fate, in every probability the system of which they form a part would collapse with them. The brokers may not be essential to the system, but it is always dangerous to "swop horses whilst crossing a stream."

In 1865 Overend, Gurney & Co. converted their business into a joint stock company for the same reason that some private firms adopt the procedure—because their profits were decreasing—though this was not known until after the crash of 1866. During the panic of 1857 the Bank of England made large advances to Overends; but when, early in May, 1866, the firm again applied to the Bank for assistance, the request was refused. It has been suggested that the Bank's decision was prompted by malevolence, but at so crucial a moment the directors of the Bank would have hesitated to make a rod for their own backs, and, had they believed in the genuineness of Overends' application, they would have gladly granted the accommodation in order to spare themselves the panic which they knew must follow their refusal to assist a firm with liabilities of over £19,000,000. Moreover, subsequent events confirmed the judgment of the directors of the Bank of England.

When the partners of Overend, Gurney & Co. discovered that their books were full of possible bad debts, they promptly converted the firm into a company, guaranteed the book debts, and appointed directors. Shortly afterwards it was noticed that the Gurneys were realising their property, and suspicion was at once aroused, for it was naturally assumed that they had incurred heavy losses. When, therefore, the company appealed to the Bank the next year, the directors were sceptical, for though Overends still retained the entire confidence of their country customers, there undoubtedly existed a feeling of distrust in the City, and the directors of the Bank of England shared in the opinion there prevailing.

When the rash speculations of the partners were disclosed the public was loud in its abuse, and nothing short of a prosecution would satisfy it; and when, early in January, 1869, the directors of Overends were committed for trial on the gravest of charges, the crowd manifested its delight. But the comedy followed. The trial took place at the end of the year, by which time public opinion had completely veered round, and when it became known that the accused were acquitted, this same crowd cheered lustily. Small wonder that a Government, which must be well aware of the vagaries of crowds, should hesitate to conduct a public prosecution.

The panic of 1866, though the suspension of the Bank Act immediately brought relief, dealt a fearful blow to credit, and the country recovered from the shock with painful slowness. Foreigners, alarmed by the disorganisation of the London money market, began to withdraw their capital, and the Bank, in order to check this drain of gold outwards, was compelled to keep its discount rate at ten per cent. for three weary months.

By the middle of 1867 the Bank rate was at two per cent.; but even the company promoter had not the audacity to show himself, so depressed was the public spirit by the disasters of the previous year. The great railway companies, too, began to find themselves in financial straits, and their credit was so bad that they could only raise money on debenture stocks at high rates of interest, for the public then looked upon their ordinary shares as distinctly speculative holdings. As the railway directors neglected to borrow with the option of redemption at certain figures at a future date, it followed that, when their credit greatly improved at a later period, the companies were saddled with a huge drain in the shape of high interest on their debenture issues, whereas, had their directors exercised ordinary prudence, they would now be paying very much less upon their prior stocks, and consequently the dividends on their ordinary shares would be proportionately greater. Evidently, then, the interests of the shareholders were sacrificed to the holders of the debenture and preferred stocks.

As the prior stocks absorb so large a share of the profits, and, moreover, as the amount so absorbed is practically always the same, whereas the revenue is variable, it follows that the distributions on the ordinary shares fluctuate considerably. This fact, of course, has not escaped speculators, who work out the ratio of ordinary share capital to total capital; and the smaller the ratio the more inconstant will be the dividends, and the greater the movement in prices. Investors know that, should the trade of the country be improving rapidly, a certain railway will earn more; and if its share capital ratio be small, then the increase in revenue will largely swell the ordinary dividends thereupon—so they speculate for a rise.

The Franco-German war, which broke out in 1870 did not at first exercise any very great effect on the English money market, for though the Bank raised its rate to six per cent. on the 4th August that year, it was at two and a half before the end of September. Indeed, after the panic of 1866 down to the middle of 1870, scarcely a ripple disturbed the unusual calm of the money market, but the three crises since 1844 were largely accountable for that. They taught both Lombard Street and the Bank of England that caution is essential to the successful working of our banking system, and that fair reserves, however great the loss of interest incurred thereupon, are indispensable to a banker. The result of these bitter lessons may be read in the comparatively peaceful history of English banking since 1866.

In 1870 specie payments were temporarily suspended by the Bank of France, and the European demand for the precious metals had to be met by the Bank of England. A much larger amount of foreign capital, consequently, was deposited in London, which then became the Clearing House of Europe, and the accumulation of so much foreign money unquestionably made the money market more sensitive, and increased the responsibilities of the Bank, whose store in the Issue Department was then peculiarly exposed to the danger of a drain outwards.

The Franco-German war ended disastrously for France in 1871, and the vanquished had to pay a huge indemnity to the victor. France paid considerable sums to Germany by bills on England, and although Germany employed a certain proportion of the capital so obtained in the London money market, it withdrew large sums in gold, which were required for purposes of currency reform. During the latter part of 1872 the Bank rates were decidedly high, and in November, 1873, nine per cent. was recorded for about two weeks, but by December it was down to four and a half again. The Bank, no doubt, had its anxious moments during this period, for the larger the drain outwards the more dependent would be the bill brokers upon it, and the directors could not refuse to increase their advances to the brokers, because, had they done so, there would have been a panic at once.

We can now see distinctly how our system works. First, we get the bill brokers or middlemen, who, from the nature of their business, cannot afford to keep reserves, because their margin of profit is so small; and secondly there are the bankers, who keep their reserves with the Bank of England, which is thereby placed, so to speak, in the centre of the money market.

The Bank, after it was stripped of its monopoly of joint stock banking, failed for a time to understand its new environment, and it would have closed its doors three times since 1844 but for Government intervention, viz., in 1847, 1857, and 1866. However, when we remember that its directors were merchants, not trained bankers, and that the Bank had to adapt itself to entirely changed surroundings, this result is not remarkable. So little acquainted were the directors with the laws of banking that they actually believed the Act of 1844 would prove a panacea for all kinds of financial troubles; but their eyes were opened very widely indeed in 1847, and they gradually came to the common-sense conclusion that "the higher the ratio of reserve in the Banking Department the smaller is the danger of disaster to the Bank and to the country."

During 1866 the Bank was fairly well prepared, and, for the first time in its history, it met a panic in a scientific or common-sense manner, and advanced without hesitation to all would-be borrowers whose securities were good. The greatest danger the Bank has to face is the suspension or stoppage of the credit machine of which it is the heart, for if the progress of that machine be arrested, then the trade of the country must also stop, and England will be bankrupt.

So long as the machine can be kept in motion a catastrophe is impossible, and experience has taught the Bank that, during a period of pronounced distrust, this can only be done by advancing liberally against certain securities, and by a skilful use of the "Bank rate." The whole credit machine must work smoothly, and it would be madness, at such a moment, for the Bank to attempt to leave any part of the machine (the bill brokers for instance) to its fate. This is now fully recognised, and consequently a better feeling exists between the various divisions of the money market.

The credit machine is kept in motion by the workshops; therefore, during a panic money has to be advanced to discount good trade bills in order to support the workshops, for if a rumour got about that the banks were refusing the acceptances of strong firms, the pressure to borrow would immediately increase, thereby adding a fresh danger to the situation, and causing nervous depositors to rush in a body to the banks for their money.

It follows, therefore, that in order to arrest a panic, and to prevent a dangerous run upon their resources, the banks must lend freely to strong clients. In a time of financial stress the weak go to the wall, for finance is no exception to the rule that only the strong can live when a storm bursts and causes a struggle for existence. There is no room for sentiment at such a moment. The fight is bitter and to the finish. Sentiment comes in afterwards. This state of affairs is one of the curious products of modern civilisation, and, if you want to alter it, you must first alter human nature, which changes strangely little as the centuries roll on.

At first sight these sudden advances seem highly imprudent, because the banks are parting with their resources, but unless the workshops are assisted the banks *must* break: whereas, by advancing liberally on the best securities at high rates of interest, the dangerous element is speedily weeded out, and, provided the reserves of the banks are fairly large in proportion to their liabilities, a healthy reaction is practically certain to assert itself long before the end of their lending power is reached. The Bank, when it advances, of course creates credit in its books, and so adds to the resources of Lombard Street. The relief thus obtained is artificial, and, were it intended as a permanent cure of a disease, it must in the end only aggravate the malady. But it is temporary assistance during a trying time that the workshops require, and it is just this which our modern credit system, when skilfully administered, can give admirably. In fact it possesses the very machinery for the purpose. This sudden demand for additional credit (not specie) during a period of pronounced distrust is fortunately of short duration, and the Bank is, therefore, only called upon to make large loans for a short time, as, though the depression following a panic may prove lasting, the acute stage which the Bank has to face is soon over.

The dangers of our credit system are apparent to everybody; but when critics point to the panics which have occurred since the Act was passed, and make deductions therefrom to the effect that the Bank may find itself in a similar plight should another such whirlwind develop, they usually forget that, though the same danger exists, our banking companies are now much more prudently managed, and that the directors of the Bank of England, having the misfortunes of the past to guide them, are thoroughly acquainted with the delicacy of the machine they manage, and are, consequently, less liable to err.

We have seen that the joint stock banking movement began in 1826 under conditions which were far from favourable, and the companies, like the Bank of England itself, having to learn their business as the movement progressed, naturally committed many blunders; but when the dangers of banking were better understood failures became much less frequent, and after 1866 they were few and far between. The credit of the joint stock banks vastly improved in consequence, and confidence in their stability soon began to take the place of distrust. But in 1878 the failure of the City of Glasgow Bank and of the West of England Bank, together with some half-dozen private bankers and banking companies, undoubtedly revived old prejudices and created a feeling of unrest among depositors and shareholders.

The City of Glasgow Bank, it will be remembered, was in trouble during 1857, but in 1878 both its customers and shareholders had reason to regret that it ever opened its doors again, for the gravest irregularities were disclosed when its affairs were examined, false balance sheets having been certified by auditors and directors during a period of over four years; and once again the public was startled out of its sense of security by the discovery that some bank directors and auditors were not less peccant than the majority of the human race when hazardous speculations landed them in financial difficulties.

The directors of the City of Glasgow Bank finding themselves out of their depth, clutched at the proverbial straw, and, like a weak individual who starts with the best of intentions, they were speedily sucked into the vortex of crime. By the Act of 1845 the directors were bound to hold gold against any excess in the amount of the bank's circulation fixed thereby, but they overcame this difficulty by the simple expedient of making false returns to the Government. Having once crossed the line which separates the sheep from the goats the rest was easy.

With an utter disregard for the interests of the shareholders, the directors advanced huge sums to firms in which they were pecuniarily interested, and, as these firms did badly, they were compelled either to bolster them up with additional loans or to allow them to fail. They chose the latter alternative, and, as might have been expected, the bank's assets rapidly dwindled, millions of pounds in the shape of bad debts being disguised on the right hand side of the balance sheet as cash in hand, Government securities, and so on. The business of the bank soon degenerated into a mere gamble, and during the latter part of its career the institution was only kept in existence by the continuous perpetration of frauds.

Of course the longer the game (it can be dignified by no other name) continued the more desperate were the efforts it called forth, and just before the end the directors hit upon the brilliant idea of conducting a big gamble in Australia, in the vain hope that a decided success would obliterate the mistakes of the past; but about this time rumour was active, and when it was noticed that the bank's acceptances were being hawked all over the City, holders of its paper became suspicious. The bill brokers naturally do not like putting all their eggs in one basket, but endeavour to get as many good names as possible, so that, should a particular firm meet with misfortune, they may be in a position to bear the loss. When, therefore, the City of Glasgow Bank's paper was offered freely, they refused to place more of its bills in their cases, and, inquiries concerning the bank being made in consequence, the end soon came.

Though the revelations which followed generated a feeling of intense nervousness among bank shareholders and depositors both in Scotland and this country, and undoubtedly caused a slight panic, the country was spared a crisis. The Scotch banks, in order to prevent the run extending to themselves, encashed the notes of the delinquent institution, and advanced liberally to those persons whose money and securities were held by the City of Glasgow Bank. In this manner a serious panic was averted.

The Bank of England raised its rate immediately danger was threatened, and on the 14th October, 1878, the rate touched six per cent., but it fell to five per cent. in November, and money was exceptionally cheap during the next two years. The West of England Bank had also advanced its resources in a reckless manner, and it failed badly in consequence; but the Scotch scandals were not repeated, and the public gradually regained confidence in the banking companies.

When it was clearly seen after the failure of the Glasgow Bank, how easily a large bank, unless it be most cautiously and prudently managed, can ruin its members and customers, the public hesitated to hold shares in an unlimited banking company. For a time the prices of bank shares fell considerably, and fiction became tediously full of heroines and heroes who lost their fortunes by holding just one share in the Glasgow Bank. It was the "just one share" that proved so thrilling, and accentuated the sadness and the danger of possessing shares in an unlimited bank. The risks of a banking business were discussed on every side; and, after this failure, the unlimited banking companies took steps which enabled them to affix the desirable word "limited" to their registered names.

From the time of the failures of the City of Glasgow Bank and the West of England Bank until 1890, when the Baring crisis suddenly opened the eyes of the public to the dangerous gamble which was taking place in South American securities, the money market enjoyed a period of comparative calm. Speculation since 1885 had increased in volume, and the prices of securities steadily rose; but early in 1890 it became apparent that continuous speculation had inflated prices and created a situation which could not last. The Bank rate during the autumn of 1889 was exceptionally high, and remained at six per cent. from 30th December, 1889, to 20th February, 1890, when it gradually descended, but this fall only proved the lull before the storm, which raged furiously in the November following.

England has always speculated largely in both North and South America, and the result has almost invariably been a panic. In 1890 it was the Argentine Republic which was to prove an Eldorado for the British investor, and Baring Brothers were so convinced that this wonderful land must prove a veritable gold mine that they practically staked the existence of their firm upon it, but Argentina sadly disappointed its backers. Having staked their all and lost, there were many who thought that Barings should have paid the penalty of their mistake, for Fate certainly was not so kind to some of the smaller losers in the gamble as was the Bank of England to Baring Brothers.

In June the Buenos Ayres Western Railway was unable to raise capital in this country; and when at a later date Baring Brothers failed to place a new Argentine loan, the worst was feared. Earlier in the year the United States had increased its circulation of silver currency, thereby creating a sudden demand for that metal and a proportionate rise in those securities upon which the interest is payable in silver. A fall soon followed; and when it was found that the Argentine Government was in straits, Stock Exchange settlements became difficult. The banks, which had advanced huge sums to the Stock Exchange on American securities, increased their margins directly the markets looked dangerous; consequently high rates of interest, together with the rapid fall in South American securities, made "carrying over" in the House an expensive operation. Speculators became alarmed, and sold out at panic prices in order to cut their losses, and on 7th November pressure upon the Bank of England became so great that the rate was raised from five to six per cent.

Lord Revelstoke, who was a partner in the firm of Baring Brothers, was also a director of the Bank of England, and, finding that his firm was in difficulties, he disclosed his position to the Bank directors, who, when they heard that Messrs. Barings' liabilities to the public amounted to over £28,000,000, felt that even the Bank of England could not afford to guarantee so large a sum; so, after much deliberation, it was decided to invite the co-operation of Lombard Street in the bolstering up of Barings, and, for the first time in its history, the directors of our large banking institutions met the directors of the Bank in their sacred parlour to discuss what steps should be taken in order to avoid a disturbance of credit which, should the suspension of Barings be announced, would probably produce a crisis even more disastrous than that caused by the Overend and Gurney crash in 1866.

The resources of Lombard Street combined are infinitely greater than those of the Bank, which, we have seen, largely draws its own power therefrom, and the directors of the Bank of England, in consulting with the directors of the joint stock banks, proved that they thoroughly understood the constitution of the money market. Moreover, this new step created a precedent which bound the whole market more closely together, for each division clearly recognised how essential it is that the great machine should work smoothly. This can only be accomplished by the best of feeling existing between its constituent parts, and the wise step taken by the directors of the Bank in November, 1890, undoubtedly generated a feeling of sympathy which had formerly been noticeably absent between the various sections of the money market, and which augurs well for the harmonious working of the system in the future. Such sympathy may be the outcome of enlightened selfishness, but it is none the less valuable.

The directors of the joint stock banks, when the position of Baring Brothers was revealed to them, instantly recognised the danger of the position, and, as their advances to the Stock Exchange were considerable, they were naturally anxious to prevent a catastrophe which would create a panic in the House, and the end of which it was impossible to foresee.

Barings, who are financiers in the English sense of the word, not bankers, had at the worst only been guilty of imprudent speculation, and, as all inquiries were answered in the most straightforward manner, Lombard Street was as anxious as the Old Lady herself to assist Baring Brothers over the stile. Undoubtedly Lombard Street would have liked to make an example of the firm that was caught short of cash, but it was afraid to leave it to its fate, because it knew that discrimination is not one of the characteristics of excited depositors, and that, were Barings to close their doors, the credit of Lombard Street would next be questioned.

The outcome of the meeting at the Bank was that the Bank of England agreed to make advances to Baring Brothers in order to enable them to meet their liabilities as they matured, and the large banking companies, on their side, guaranteed the Bank against loss to the extent of £15,000,000.

Immense sums had been invested in South America, and when it was rumoured that the wealthy firm of Barings was tottering, Argentine securities were practically unsaleable on the Stock Exchange, where a state of panic prevailed. For a few days the wildest rumours were noised abroad, and the tension, just at the height of the panic, became so acute that even the Consol market was idle. The market then turned in despair to the Bank, which was compelled to borrow £3,000,000 from the Bank of France as a precautionary measure, and also to accept help from the Russian Government.

The British Government, fully alive to the gravity of the Bank's position, promised to suspend the Act in case of need; but when it became known that Barings were to be supported, and that the Bank of England was lending freely on approved securities at high rates of interest, confidence was restored, though a few days earlier it had looked as if a dangerous crisis were imminent. The Bank Act, however, was not suspended, but it is difficult to say what might have happened had not the Bank of France come to the rescue, for the gold advanced by that institution at so awkward a time doubtless tended to greatly alleviate the feeling of apprehension which existed in this country, and which, at any moment, might have overcome restraint.

The Bank rate remained at six per cent. until 4th December (a period of twenty-seven days), when it was reduced to five per cent.; for the high rates ruling in the market attracted gold to this country, and increased the reserve of the Bank of England beyond the apprehension minimum, thereby enabling that institution to make the change in question. By the middle of the following year (1891) the Bank's rate of discount was down to two-and-a-half per cent.; but confidence was not restored for some considerable time; and we all remember the deadly dull years of 1894 and 1895, when it was predicted that Consols would never again fall below 100. The financial prophets and the weather prophets are generally wrong, but though we have acquired the habit of tapping the glass each morning, a prudent man carries his umbrella all the same.

The directors of the Bank of England, when they were informed of Baring Brothers' position, acted with great tact and ability. They did not hesitate to assist everybody who possessed good securities, and when it was found that loanable capital was obtainable, the alarming symptoms which were at first in evidence soon subsided. Whether or not the Bank were sufficiently prepared at the time is, however, a matter of opinion. The directors certainly began the year badly, for the ratio of the reserve in the Banking Department was under twenty-eight per cent.—a dangerously low proportion in these times, when huge sums of foreign capital may be suddenly withdrawn from the market at the least sign of discredit. Nor are high rates of discount always effective in immediately attracting gold to the Bank, as the Bank of France, should it desire to retain its bullion, can always charge a prohibitive premium on its gold. Certainly, since 1890 the Bank of England has maintained larger reserves, and the Baring panic unquestionably proved that such a step was necessary.

It would seem that the panic of 1890 was the result of a Stock Exchange gamble, which was only rendered possible by the large loans on securities made to members of the House by the banks. The Baring incident brought matters to a climax, and Lombard Street, which was more involved in the speculation than many persons imagined, had to save both that firm and the Stock Exchange in order to avoid a crop of bad debts, which, with numerous failures, and a far greater drop in the prices of securities, would have inevitably resulted.

Mr. Lidderdale, who was Governor of the Bank during this period, acted with great energy, and after the danger was passed congratulations were showered upon him from every side.

The Stock Exchange presented an address to Mr. Lidderdale, and in making the presentation its spokesman said: "If the Bank had not acted in the way it did, a great disaster would have befallen the mercantile community." Yes, and that disaster would have been largely caused by speculation on the Stock Exchange. Further, had not the directors of the Bank met this incipient panic in a scientific manner, and used their power as precedent dictated, members of the House would have failed by the dozen. One is forced to the conclusion that Lombard Street and the Stock Exchange had a lucky escape, and that the "members of the mercantile community" were the unfortunates who, after years of toil, had to wipe out the deficit.

Now we come to the bright side of the picture. Later on the business of Baring Brothers was converted into a company, and in 1895 it was definitely announced that the assets of the firm had been liquidated without any loss whatsoever to the guarantors. Baring Brothers & Co., Limited, now publish a strong balance sheet, which entitles the company to a place among our well-managed institutions, and so short is the memory of the public when things financial are in question, that the panic of 1890 is, if not quite forgotten, at least regarded as ancient history. Indeed, the public hardly seems to realise that, in November, 1890, the monetary situation was so acute that a quickening of the public pulse would probably have resulted in one of the most dangerous crises the country has ever been called upon to face.

After the Baring crisis the market was unperturbed for a little while, but in 1893 many of the Australian banks found themselves in difficulties, and as the people in this country, tempted by the high rates offered at the London offices of the Australian banks, and by their agents on this side, had deposited largely with them, a very bitter feeling soon manifested itself. Australia, like South America, was to prove an Eldorado for the small investor, but the pace was forced, and the reaction came in 1893, when many of the banks suspended payment. Even now some of the Australian banks in London are not any too strong, and discrimination is certainly desirable.

On 9th October, 1899, the Boers issued their famous Ultimatum, to which they immediately received an answer that was brief and unmistakeable; but, unfortunately, the pen of the Government at first proved mightier than the sword, and by 3rd November White was shut up in Ladysmith. Then followed the failures of Methuen and Gatacre, and on 15th December General Buller was repulsed at Colenso. Thoroughly roused, the Government sent out Lord Roberts and Lord Kitchener. On the night of 6th January, 1900, the Boers made a desperate attempt to take Ladysmith, while Buller again failed to relieve the town on the 22nd, and did not enter it until after Cronje was brought to bay at Paardeberg at the end of February.

This period of disaster cast a gloom over the whole nation, which grew sullen and determined, and, when at last the tide began to turn, the sudden lifting of the burden immediately metamorphosed a silent depressed crowd into a cheering multitude, which on Mafeking day turned London into a veritable pandemonium; but the depression caused by unpleasant surprises was intense, and, therefore, the joy at finding the incubus gone was the more irrepressible. Hence the disorderly scenes upon the day in question. A reaction after the period of suspense was inevitable, and the greater the gloom the more violent would be the excitement that followed when the first ray of sunshine pierced the mist. Yet how little was this understood at the time.

That financial barometer—the Bank rate—began to reflect the political situation early in October. Our state of unpreparedness was a by-word on the Continent, and when in September, 1899, the Boers displayed an unyielding attitude, which was at first mistaken for bravado, our overweening confidence in the British soldier blinded our eyes to the imperfections of our fighting machine. The Continent, which was better informed than the British Government, believed that the Boers were determined. On the 3rd October, when the Free State burghers occupied Van Reenen's Pass, the Bank advanced its rate to four-and-a-half per cent.; on the 5th October the rate was five per cent., and on the 30th November six per cent., where it remained until the 11th January, 1900, when five per cent. was recorded.

But if the Government was unprepared the Bank of England was not, and from start to finish, by a judicious use of its rate of discount, an adequate supply of bullion was maintained in the Issue Department. Long experience had taught its lesson, and our financial machine, which was in a good state of preparedness, worked without a hitch. Who can doubt that if our fighting machine had been as ably handled, it would have done its work well from first to last?

There is also another point which is well worth attention. If our banks neglect to keep good reserves, a panic results immediately there is any unusual demand upon their resources, and the cost of a panic soon convinces their directors that it is cheaper to be always prepared. Will the expenditure of some £230,000,000 teach the Government the same simple truth? If we must have an army, it is madness not to keep it—as our banks are kept—ready. Mr. Kruger and his advisers did not consider the latent potentiality of the British fighting machine. They ascertained its state of preparedness to strike at a moment's notice, and, seeing that it was unprepared, the Boers wisely struck the first blow, hoping to drive the English into the sea before the machine could be adapted to a new environment. On the other hand, they failed to realise the resources of the Empire. Had the Boers believed that the British could land an army of even 150,000 men in South Africa, in all probability there would have been no war. The Government, which was caught unprepared, had to pour out money like water, because it had neglected to take one of the simplest business precautions—to keep the army ready.

On 31st May, 1902, peace was declared, and now the country has to face a domestic problem. In 1899 trade was good, and in 1900 the prices of commodities were at their zenith; but during 1901 a reaction set in, and at the present time trade is certainly not active. Reservists are arriving from South Africa in large numbers; and, as the labour market is already depressed, a number of them are sure to experience considerable difficulty in finding employment. War is certainly not a business that civilises, and if a man has once tasted blood, in however just a cause, it is difficult to believe that life will seem quite so sacred to him again. Should the times become really bad, these men who have returned from the front, and who cannot again find a place in civil life, will turn instinctively to the weapons upon which they have learned to depend. Consequently, should there be a severe depression in trade, an epidemic of crime is one of those possibilities which may send a thrill of horror through the country.

Since September, 1899, the money market has certainly had to contend with great difficulties, and a system which has proved itself more than equal to the strain surely cannot be so undesirable as certain critics would have us believe. Again, the more the public understands the system, the less is the danger of panic; for it must be apparent to every man who reads this book that, if he study his own interests, he will select a strong bank, and, having taken that precaution, he will carefully refrain from rushing for his deposit during a time of stress.

CHAPTER XVI.
THE BANKS AND THE PUBLIC.

WE have seen that the history of the Bank of England may be divided into two periods. From 1708 to 1826 the Bank enjoyed the monopoly of joint stock banking in England. After 1826 it had to adapt itself to a constantly changing environment. England, in fact, outgrew the Bank, just as the financial world has outgrown London. The directors of the Bank of England were City merchants, whose ideas usually run in a particular groove. It is not, therefore, in the least remarkable that they stuck to old customs and neglected new opportunities. The directors of the London and Westminster Bank made the same mistake. So did those of the Union Bank of London, the London Joint Stock Bank, and one or two others, simply because their training was of the City: that is to say, like the streets around the Bank, narrow.

To a very great extent the Bank of England is dependent upon the bankers' balances, for, unless it held them, it would not be able to finance the Government. If its directors had, however, thoroughly understood the movement of 1826, the Bank would now be a much more independent institution, and would be a power in every county in England and Wales. In 1826 the Government expressly desired the directors of the Bank to open country branches, and by 1830 it possessed eleven offices in the large provincial towns. But the innovation was not encouraged by those in authority, and to-day the Bank of England possesses only nine country and two Metropolitan branches. Unquestionably a golden opportunity was neglected, for, had the directors decided to open in the large provincial towns, Bank stock would probably be worth over five hundred at this moment.

At first the joint stock bank movement was neither popular nor successful, but nobody questioned the credit of the Bank of England; and if that institution had quickly met the wants of the country by opening branches in the towns, it could have had the pick of the provincial business, for everybody, including both commercial firms and the leisured classes, would have been anxious to deal with a bank which was absolutely above suspicion. And who would dream of making a run upon the "Government" bank? The Bank would gradually have accumulated vast deposits, which would have made it independent of the "bankers' balances"; but the ground is now covered with banking companies, and the Bank of England's opportunity is gone, never to return. At present it is a great bank of discount. Had it farmed the provinces in earnest, it would have become a great deposit bank, deriving its power from its depositors and the Government account, instead of from the Government and the bankers, as it now does. But its directors were not trained bankers, and they failed to realise the important part that branches or feeders were to play in the new system, consequently, with the huge capital of the Bank, large dividends on its stock are now out of the question.

Our present system is, after all, the result of chance as well as of skill. It grew. Further it committed all the follies of youth and inexperience. Then, again, at the beginning, it was as a house divided against itself, and consequently upon more than one occasion it fell, for a banking system can only be worked successfully when all the strong members are pledged either to stand or to fall together. Indeed, our system would be considerably strengthened if the great banks were in closer touch with the Bank of England.

Some few years ago, when there was a somewhat bitter feeling between Lombard Street and the Bank, it was often suggested that were each bank to keep its own reserve of cash the rate of discount would be more stable; but, in the event of such a change, the banks would undoubtedly have to maintain increased reserves, and a greater proportion of their resources would consequently be non-productive. As they would then have less capital to lend, it also follows that, even if rates in the open market did fluctuate less, the average rate of discount paid by the public would be higher, because there would be less capital in the London short loan money market to meet the demands of the bill brokers and stockbrokers.

On the other hand, if the banks realised their investments in proportion as they increased their reserves, and so maintained the same amount of capital in the London short loan fund, their own profits would decrease; and the bank proprietors are not philanthropists. In the one case the public would suffer, and in the other the banks themselves would lose, whilst in neither instance is the advantage to be gained at all proportionate to the risk incurred by a sudden disturbance of credit.

Our present system, with all its imperfections, has gradually grown up around the Bank of England, and if Lombard Street were to decide to keep its own reserve, the result would be confusion, and confusion might be followed by panic—so great is the faith of the public in the Old Lady, whose history entitles her to both consideration and respect. The change might, or might not, result in a run upon Lombard Street; but the Bank of England, whether or not the money market were disorganised, would not lose the confidence of the nation, which is convinced that the Bank cannot fail.

Lombard Street, we may rest assured, would not risk so drastic a change. It may be urged that, were the banks to keep their own reserves, the Bank could not finance the Government, which would then have to borrow to a greater extent in the open market; and perhaps such would be the case. But though the Bank of England is at present largely dependent upon the "bankers' balances," and upon the power derived from its position in the centre of the system, it must not be assumed, even if the banks could agree among themselves as to the ratio of cash each should hold, that the Bank would be compelled to bow to their decision.

As a matter of fact, such a decision on the part of Lombard Street would change the Bank of England from a discount bank into a deposit bank—a metamorphosis which Lombard Street could not face with equanimity. The Bank, whatever arrangements it may make with its own customers, does not at present compete against Lombard Street for deposits at interest; but were the bankers to withdraw their balances, the Bank would be compelled to appeal to the public for deposits, and who can doubt that it could not attract as much capital to its vaults as it required? The Bank would only have to make its rate of interest sufficiently attractive, and the public would rush to it with deposits. Where would Lombard Street be then?

Unless the Bank rate be unusually high, the banks allow one-and-a-half per cent. below it upon money left at interest in London. The country deposit rate, which is somewhat higher, is affected to a certain extent by competition in the provincial towns and cities. But the Bank would not confine its efforts to London if its hand were forced. It would offer high rates at its branches, and might even open fresh offices. The bankers' deposit rates would then be forced upwards in order to arrest the drain from themselves to the Bank of England. No; Lombard Street cannot play fast and loose with the Old Lady; and, if certain critics will reflect, they will see that the Bank has less to fear from a change in our present system than have those who occasionally threaten her. Her position, were the banks foolish enough to withdraw their balances, is not quite so hopeless as it is sometimes made to appear upon paper. Indeed, the better the understanding between the Bank and Lombard Street, the safer is our "one reserve" system, and consequently the less liable is the country to financial crises—for it is only by the united action of all the great banks that the situation can be saved in times of stress. This was clearly proved during the Baring scare of 1890.

The "clearing" bankers from time to time fix the deposit rate for London by the Bank rate, and though their country branches are not bound by their decision—which is advertised in the newspapers directly a change is made—the country deposit rate fluctuates with the Bank rate, though, as a rule, it neither falls so low as the London rate when capital is cheap, nor advances so far when it is dear. Further, the rates charged for loans and advances should be regulated to a certain extent by the Bank rate. However, that is a question which need not be entered into here.

Should the bankers decide to keep their own reserves, it is evident that the Bank of England's rate of discount would immediately cease to be a representative rate, and that a powerful rival, with a great history and a clean record, would at once begin to compete against the bankers for both deposits and advances. Were the Bank of England, so to speak, to decide to remain outside the system, Lombard Street could not even fix a minimum deposit rate for London, because the Bank, if it required capital, would bid against its rivals, and would soon obtain all it needed. Instead of being more stable, rates in the open market would move up and down with startling suddenness. Would-be borrowers, puzzled by such irritating movements, would soon grow nervous, for the prices of commodities would fluctuate too, and everybody would be afraid to make large purchases. The closer one examines the question, the more absurd appears the suggestion of a split between the Bank and our great joint stock banking companies; and the only wonder is that any person with the slightest sense of proportion can seriously advance so dangerous a proposition, which that friend of our youth, "Euclid," would have at once pronounced "absurd."

Custom has placed its seal upon our banking system; and the person who is rash enough to break that seal may discover that he has released new forces, which, though theory plainly demonstrates that they will act in a certain direction, are pretty sure to make their way through an unsuspected flaw which offers less resistance. A system which has been over two hundred years in the building cannot be changed in a day—especially a system which, even if it be not understood, has entered into the daily life of the people. It is because the system is not understood that the change would be so dangerous—so irritating. It would be asking the British public to think, to change its habits, to suddenly adopt new ideas; and as that mysterious body has never yet been educated up to thinking for itself, it would be found that it would kick against a new system like the stubborn donkey it is. Here is the real danger. The change, if the public would adapt itself to it, might prove beneficial—but the public would not; and as even its advantages over the present system are doubtful, where is the practical banker who would suggest the move? His one aim is not to disturb the money market, and for that reason alone he would hesitate to remove the Bank of England from its position in the centre of the system; but when we remember that the Bank, by accepting deposits, could probably beat Lombard Street at its own game, the change in question need not be discussed seriously.

There is one other phase in modern banking which, perhaps, calls for notice, and that is the fierce competition for safe business taking place between the banks themselves both in London and the provinces. Most of our large towns and cities are overbanked. Consequently, the public has a choice of many markets, as it were; and, quite naturally, it tries to lend in the dearest and to borrow in the cheapest. It may be asked: How much longer will this state of affairs exist? And the answer is: Just so long as the banks decide that it shall; and not a day longer!

The better the risks of banking are understood by the public the more difficult will it be for a weak bank to attract custom; and as the smaller banks, especially in the manufacturing centres, are unable to obtain sufficient deposits to meet the demands for advances, it follows that, when their loans grow out of all proportion to their resources, they are compelled to amalgamate with a large institution possessing numerous branches, and therefore in a position to collect huge sums of loanable capital, and distribute it just where it is wanted.

For instance, a large bank collects very much more capital in certain districts than it lends therein; but at branches situated in busy manufacturing cities the demand for capital, especially when trade is brisk, approximates much too closely to the sums collected at those branches to be compatible with sound banking. However, the bank has accumulated more than it requires in other towns, and is therefore in a position to transfer the surplus to those places where demand is strong, and, at the same time, to maintain a good ratio of liquid assets to liabilities, whereas a local bank in a busy centre can often only meet the requirements of its customers by advancing to a dangerous extent.

The directors of such banking companies are beginning to realise this danger; and fearful that one day they may be caught short of cash, the smaller joint stock banks are gradually being absorbed by the greater companies, whose numerous tentacles enable them to distribute their capital evenly throughout their system, and to maintain fair cash reserves against their liabilities.

As the small banks disappear, competitors are removed from the market; and there is every probability that banking in this country will by-and-by be in the hands of a few large and powerful banking companies. The public could not resist the banks were they to unite against it. Already the "clearing" banks have fixed the deposit rate for London, and it is only one step farther to declare the minimum rate at which they will advance—for what resistance can the public offer to a combination with more than £910,000,000 in deposits alone behind it?

Were the banks to hold a conference, and to decide that competition must be kept within bounds, the public would not have a voice in the matter. The English banks, like those of Scotland, would, after having come to some arrangement among themselves, meet from time to time in order to fix the minimum rates of interest and commission, and their customers would either have to pay those rates or else obtain accommodation outside the confederation. Of course, all the banks would have to close up their ranks before this arrangement would be possible, and, at the moment of writing, it seems improbable that certain companies, which make a business of competition, could be persuaded to come inside. So long as the banks are divided the public will be able to drive bargains with them, but, directly they fall into line, their rule will begin, and the quicker the smaller companies disappear the nearer the reign of the banks approaches.

Seeing that our banking system can only work smoothly so long as both Lombard Street and Threadneedle Street work in harmony, it follows that in time the link which connects the large banking companies will become stronger, and the relations between them pleasanter, because, in business as elsewhere, friendship is centred in the head rather than in the heart. The banks must draw closer together, because, if they do not, their system is unworkable; and, as they are now compelled to adopt certain precautions in order to protect themselves against panic on the part of their customers (who in that respect are their enemies), it is only natural that they should take steps to put an end to excessive competition, which weakens their position and prevents their acting together at a moment when united action alone can restore confidence in their ability to meet their liabilities.

We all know the stale apothegm: "Self-preservation is the first law of nature." It is the religion of the world. We can see the law at work among our friends, but, being polite, we refrain from comment—though if we be wise, we reflect; for here is the great unpreached gospel which governs the actions of men. Self-preservation clearly dictates that the banks cannot afford to allow competition among themselves to weaken the system upon which their safety depends; and, should the danger become pronounced, they are certain to combine against the public in order to at least agree to certain minimum rates below which none will do business.

It may be said: You yourself were the first to point out that certain customers are in a position to make terms with the bankers, and to advise them to do so. That is true enough; and so long as the banks are divided amongst themselves this is possible; but it by no means follows that, because the customers can make certain bargains this year, they will be able to make similar arrangements next, for the banks have their remedy, and when the right time comes they will not neglect to take it.

We have dissected that complex machine, which is called the Money Market, and of which the Bank of England is the heart. As each unit is dependent upon the strength of the whole, no bank should be allowed to trade upon the credit of the rest, for obviously it cannot exist outside the system during a time of stress unless it possess an adequate reserve of cash. Therefore each unit ought to bear its fair share of the burden when the sun is shining, and, if it refuse, it should be made to take the consequences when the storm bursts.

The closer our banking system is examined the stronger becomes the conviction that the interests of all the banks are identical, and that, therefore, if banking is to be conducted in this country with comparative safety, every bank should be compelled, either by the law of the land or by public opinion, to keep a fair reserve in legal tender against its liabilities. Further, the true interests of the banks are the same as those of the public—for the good business man is always a cautious man, and if he takes the trouble to study the risks to which a banking business is exposed, he will hardly care to place his money with a company unless it be well prepared to face those storms to which its environment peculiarly exposes it.

Under our one reserve system the banks must either stand or fall together during a crisis. The system, therefore, requires the support of all; consequently, the duties or obligations of each bank should be clearly defined, and this can only be done by an Act of Parliament or by an understanding between the banks. The closer the banks draw together the safer is our system of banking.

CHAPTER XVII.
BANK STOCK.

WHEN the trade of the country is prosperous, we expect to see banking companies paying high dividends, because rising prices stimulate borrowing on the part of the public; and, consequently, as the resources of the banks are limited, the increased demand for loanable capital sends up rates, with the result that distributions are enhanced, and that the prices of bank shares advance in sympathy with improving dividends.

We all know that there is a link which binds industries together, and that a depression in one trade, if it prove lasting, must communicate itself to the rest. Nor is this movement confined to any one nation. Therefore, when we hear that a depression exists in Germany or in any other great manufacturing country, it is a matter for regret rather than otherwise, because the goods of that country are almost certain to be exported here in large quantities.

If there be stagnation in Germany, then money will be cheap in that country, and commodities will be cheap too. Manufacturers, therefore, will be able to obtain better prices in foreign markets; consequently, German exports will increase, and prices will soon begin to fall in England. Again, depression in the States speedily makes itself felt in the English markets, which become glutted with American goods, with the result that production lessens at home, and times gradually become, as we colloquially say, "bad."

But there is one factor with which we have not reckoned, and that is time; for though after a period of prosperity prices generally fall suddenly—as, for instance, during 1901—it usually takes two or three years before production is again in full swing. In these days, when commercial ties bind the whole world so closely together, one nation cannot afford to rejoice at the misfortune of another; and when this fact is more clearly seen and is better understood, possibly large standing armies will become an unnecessary evil, for the secret of true progress is the fact that commerce and civilisation always advance together.

The Bank of England, which deals in money and credit like every other bank, is exposed to the same influences as the rest of its kind; consequently, when trade is brisk and loanable capital dear, it pays larger dividends than during the depressed portion of a cycle. The following table will illustrate the fact:—

£14,553,000 STOCK.

	1892	1893	1894	1895	1896	1897	1898	1899	1900	1901
Highest	344	343	338	336	345	351½	367	361½	349	342
Lowest	325	325	322	322½	322	326	341	325	326	319¼
Dividend % per annum 5th April	10	10	8	8	8½	10	10	10	10	10
Dividend % per annum 5th October	9½	9	8½	8½	10	10	10	10	10	10

Average Distribution, 9½ per cent.

It is at once evident that when its distributions are compared with those of the large banking companies, the Bank does not excel as a dividend-payer, and the reason, of course, is because it has to distribute its earnings over so large an amount of stock or capital; but, although it pays fluctuating dividends—which are regulated by the average rate capital may earn during any half-year—it is noticeable that, since 1899, despite the fact of dividends being maintained at ten per cent. per annum, the price of Bank stock touched lower figures than any recorded during the decade, when, according to every financial rule, prices ought to have been well maintained. Further, the shares of the joint stock banks did not exhibit this tendency to any marked extent. Why, then, should Bank stock be an exception to the rule?

The years 1894 and 1895 were distinguished by cheap money and indifferent trade, therefore we should expect to see the Bank's dividends decrease, and its stock fall in sympathy with diminishing distributions. If we glance at the table we shall see that our deductions were realised. In 1896 trade began to improve. Rising prices lessened the purchasing power of money; consequently the industrial machine required more capital *after* the rise, because a given sum would then purchase *less*. The result was an increased demand for loanable capital, which at once became dearer; and the Bank of England, together with the other banks in the country, earned more. Again, as one would have expected, dividends and stock moved up together. During 1897 the same movements were witnessed; but in 1899 Bank stock began to fall, although distributions were maintained. This deviation from rule evidently calls for explanation. Compare, for instance, the prices of the shares of the undermentioned banks during the period in question:—

	1895.	1899.	1900.	1901.	Dividend % per annum each year since 1898.
London and County—*Highest*	95½	109½	107	107	22
" " " *Lowest*	89½	103	101½	100¼	
London and Provincial—*Highest*	21¾	22½	22¾	23⅜	18
" " " *Lowest*	19¼	21	21½	20½	
London Joint Stock-*Highest*	34¼	39	37⅞	37¾	12
" " " *Lowest*	30⅞	33¼	34	34½	1900 & 1901

We can see, in the above instances, that where dividends were maintained, prices moved between much the same figures, whilst in every case a marked advance is shown on the quotations of 1895, whereas Bank stock receded further in 1901, when the dividend was ten per cent. per annum, than it did during 1895, when the distribution for the year was only eight-and-a-quarter per cent. It is this anomaly which we have to discuss. The trade of the country from 1896 to the end of 1900 was progressive, and though in 1901 a reaction set in, the large requirements of the Government, and the state of uncertainty created by the war, kept loanable capital dear. The banks, consequently, were enabled to support their huge dividends during 1901, though their being able to declare the same rates for the last half of the present year seems doubtful.

But to return to the fall in Bank stock, which, at the moment of writing, is quoted at 326. The public, so little does it understand the position of the Bank of England, still looks upon it as a Government institution; and, as though to give colour to this illusion, we find its stock quoted in the same division as "British Funds &c." By The Trustee Act, 1893, trustees, where they are not prohibited by the trust deed, may invest in Bank of England stock; and, as a result of this enactment, there is an increased demand for its stock, which consequently yields less to a buyer; yet, strictly speaking, Bank stock cannot be classed with the so-called "gilt-edged" securities, because the interest it returns is variable.

It is true that the holder does not incur any liability, and in this sense Bank stock is a much more desirable investment than shares in a joint stock bank upon which the member is liable for certain stated sums in the shape of uncalled capital; but the Government does not guarantee the dividends of the Bank. Indeed, it is only interested in the Bank of England in the same manner that a large customer is interested in his banker; and, though, in every probability, so long as the Government banks with the Old Lady, it will assist her whenever cause may arise, it is not pledged so to do. Again, the twentieth century may be productive of great change; and, though it seems improbable that a Government would remove its accounts from the Bank, such an event is by no means impossible, for the only tie between the Government and the Bank of England is that the former is the Bank's oldest client.

On the other hand, so long as Government does keep its balances at the Bank of England, it cannot afford to allow the Bank to fail, even were there the risk of it doing so. But holders of Bank stock, like the holders of shares in any other bank, would be paid last should the Bank be wound up, however remote a possibility that may be; and seeing that their capital is not a prior charge upon the assets of the Bank, and that, therefore, £100 of stock is worth £326 only so long as the Bank of England is a going concern, it is difficult to see why Bank stock should be considered a desirable holding for trustees. It seems to me that, valuable though the security undoubtedly is, it does not possess a single one of those characteristics which should distinguish a "trustee" stock, for dividends are fluctuating, and capital is a *last* charge on the assets of the Bank. In fact, the stock is a kind of guarantee to the customers—and a splendid guarantee too, for it is the Bank's large capital which makes it the safest bank for depositors in the land. But that the holders of a "trustee" stock should, in the event of a company being wound up, get the *last* look in is surely somewhat odd. However, this is only another illustration of the confidence the public has in the Bank of England, which, people are convinced, will exist as long as the nation.

The Bank, because the public imagines that it is connected more closely with the Government than in reality is the case, naturally suffers in credit when its patron does. Consequently during 1899, when the British reverses in South Africa increased the difficulties of the Government and depressed Consols, Bank stock, although dividends were maintained at ten per cent. per annum, fell in sympathy with Government securities, despite the fact that the shares of the large English banking companies were not appreciably affected. Of course this depreciation, which has proved lasting, was not the result of sound reasoning, for so long as the war continued money was sure to be dear, and dear money plainly indicated that the Bank would support its dividend of ten per cent. Further, the large Government borrowings constantly compelled the outside market to borrow from the Bank, which, had it so decided, could have charged exceptionally high rates, and thereby have added considerably to its profit; but, with its usual moderation, it wisely refrained from exacting excessive rates from those who, when Lombard Street was temporarily denuded of surplus capital, were compelled to apply to it for loans. The Bank, during the trying period in question, certainly did not attempt to make extra profit out of the nation's misfortune, as it assuredly might have done had its directors been actuated by a grasping spirit. Is there another bank in the land that would not have profited by the occasion? There may be; but I am disposed to doubt it, and I certainly should not care to attempt to name the institution.

Here, then, we find two influences at work at the same time, and the result is distinctly curious. The Bank of England, from the nature of its business, pays increased dividends when trade is good, therefore its stock should advance in value during the prosperous portion of a cycle; but, because of its business relation with the Government, its stock is looked upon by the public as a kind of Government security, and, consequently, when any political event causes Consols to fall, Bank stock recedes in sympathy with them. There is no reason for this movement, and if it proves anything it proves how little Finance is understood by the investing public. Here is a stock which pays fluctuating dividends classed with the so-called "gilt-edged" variety of securities; therefore its movements often seem erratic, because at one time it responds to the law that regulates the price of gilt-edged stocks, and at another to the law which decides the price of industrials.

It can be seen from our list that for the decade ended 1901 the Bank of England paid an average dividend of nine-and-a-half per cent. per annum. Based on the said average, a purchaser, if he require a return of three per cent. for his money, will have to buy Bank stock at 316-2/3; but 319¼ in 1901 is the lowest price it has touched since 1888, and it seems highly probable that our would-be purchaser at 316-2/3 would wait in vain for his stock at those figures. Indeed, the present price, 326, looks cheap for Bank stock. Bought at 325, and based on an average dividend of nine-and-a-half per cent., the stock would return about £2 18s. 6d. per cent. So small a return upon one's money is not calculated to make one anxious to buy, and Consols at 93 are perhaps a greater temptation, though neither investment appeals very strongly, so far as interest is concerned, to the imagination.

If purchased during the depressed portion of a cycle, the shares of the large banking companies can be bought at a price which will yield an average dividend of over four-and-a-half per cent. to the investor; but it must be borne in mind that, as a rule, he incurs a certain liability on such shares, whereas Bank stock is free from possible calls, and, consequently, not exposed to the objection which is constantly urged against the majority of bank shares as an investment.

Some of my readers, I dare say, will not agree with all my conclusions; and, perhaps, it may be urged that the information herein contained were better withheld from the general public. But the truth is always worth the telling, and if our banking system will not bear investigation then it must be a bad one. Despite obvious defects in construction, it is apparent, however, that our great credit machine, when skilfully managed, can successfully endure considerable strain; and, if gold be dangerously economised, our present system at least gives us that inestimable blessing—Cheap Money.

Milton Keynes UK
Ingram Content Group UK Ltd.
UKHW030909151124
451262UK00006B/867